Jolly Grammar 1
Teacher's Book

Daily Guidance for teaching grammar and spelling with the Jolly Grammar 1 Pupil Book

Written by

Sara Wernham and Sue Lloyd

Edited by Louise Van-Pottelsberghe

Contents

Part 1: The Jolly Grammar Programme

    Introduction   3

    Teaching Ideas for Grammar   5

    Teaching Ideas for Spelling   15

    Spelling and Grammar Lessons   23

Part 2: Daily Guidance

    Teaching with the Jolly Grammar 1 Pupil Book   31

PART 1

Introduction

For ease of use, this *Teacher's Book* has been divided into two distinct parts. The first part gives a comprehensive introduction to *Jolly Grammar* and explains the *Jolly Grammar* teaching method in detail. It is a good idea to read this part of the *Teacher's Book* before using the *Jolly Grammar 1 Pupil and Teacher's Books* in the classroom. The second part of the *Teacher's Book* provides a thorough and structured lesson plan for each day of teaching. The lesson plans in this part of the book are designed specifically for use with the corresponding pages in the *Jolly Grammar 1 Pupil Book*.

The *Jolly Grammar 1* programme follows on from the *Jolly Phonics* programme. It is designed to:

- introduce the rudiments of grammar,
- teach spelling systematically,
- improve the children's vocabulary and comprehension skills,
- reinforce the skills taught in the *Jolly Phonics Pupil Books*, and
- extend the children's phonic knowledge.

Like the activities in the *Jolly Phonics Pupil Books*, the teaching in the *Jolly Grammar 1 Pupil Book* is multisensory and active, and progresses at a challenging pace. The *Jolly Grammar 1 Pupil and Teacher's Books* are especially suitable for teaching young children. Each part of speech, for example, is introduced with an accompanying action and colour. The actions not only enliven the teaching, but also make the parts of speech easier for the children to remember. The colours, which are useful when identifying and labelling parts of speech in sentences, are the same as those used in Montessori Schools. Like the *Jolly Phonics Teacher's Book*, the *Jolly Grammar 1 Teacher's Book* explains all the essential teaching ideas and provides detailed guidance for each grammar lesson. The *Jolly Grammar 1 Pupil and Teacher's Books* can be used alone, or alongside the *Jolly Grammar Big Book 1*, which provides valuable additional support.

Children's achievement

The most dramatic improvements to result from using the *Jolly Grammar 1 Pupil and Teacher's Books* will be found in the children's writing. After completing the *Jolly Grammar 1 Pupil Book*, children will spell and punctuate more accurately, use a wider vocabulary, and have a clearer understanding of how language works.

In their first year at school, the *Jolly Phonics Pupil Books* teach the children how to write independently, by listening for the sounds in words and choosing the letters to represent the sounds. This skill enables the children to write pages of news and stories. It is a joy to read their work and to see the pride and confidence they derive from their newly-acquired skills. It is important to build upon this foundation in the following year. The *Jolly Grammar 1 Pupil and Teacher's Books* provide teaching ideas designed to develop the children's writing skills. Gradually, the children become aware that they are writing for a purpose: that their words are intended to be read and understood. They learn that their writing is easier to understand if it is grammatically correct, accurately spelt, well-punctuated and neatly written. The children also learn that, if they use interesting words, their writing can give real pleasure. Even at this early stage, it is valuable for children to have a simple understanding of this long-term goal.

The format of the Jolly Grammar 1 programme

The *Jolly Grammar 1* programme consists of a *Teacher's Book*, offering detailed lesson plans, and a corresponding *Pupil Book*, with activities for each lesson. Enough material is provided in these books for 36 weeks' teaching, with two lessons for each week. The *Jolly Grammar 1 Pupil Book* is designed so that there is one activity page for each lesson. Each lesson is intended to take up about one hours' teaching time.

Although the programme is called *Jolly Grammar*, there are in fact two elements to the programme, namely spelling and grammar. The material in the *Pupil and Teacher's Books* is organised so that the first of the weeks' lessons concentrates on spelling and the second on grammar. However, the terms are used loosely, and there is some overlap: punctuation, vocabulary development and alphabet work are among the areas covered in both spelling and grammar lessons. This is deliberate, as the two elements complement each other when combined.

The *Jolly Grammar 1* programme covers the more structured aspects of literacy, and is intended to take up only a part of the teaching time set aside for literacy work. If two days' literacy lessons are devoted to *Jolly Grammar* each week, this leaves three lessons that can be devoted to the areas not covered by *Jolly Grammar*, such as comprehension, group reading, independent and creative writing, and handwriting practice. The children should be shown how spelling and grammar relate to their other work, in comprehension exercises, reading, and independent writing. For instance, if the children have recently learnt about compound words, and there is an example of one in a poem they are studying, the children can be encouraged to spot it in the text.

For each activity page in the children's *Pupil Books* there is a corresponding page in the *Teacher's Book*, offering a detailed lesson plan and useful teaching guidance. More detailed explanations of particular topics are provided in the two following sections: *Teaching ideas for Grammar* and *Teaching ideas for Spelling*.

To avoid confusion, the *Jolly Grammar* programme follows the convention of using different parentheses to distinguish between letter names and letter sounds. Letter names are shown between these parentheses: ⟨ ⟩. For example, the word *ship* begins with the letter ⟨s⟩. By contrast, letter sounds are shown between these parentheses: / /. For example, the word *ship* begins with the /sh/ sound.

Teaching ideas for grammar

The benefits of learning grammar are cumulative. In the early stages, the children's grammar knowledge will help them to improve the clarity and quality of their writing. Later on, their grammar knowledge will help them to understand more complicated texts, learn foreign languages with greater ease, and use Standard English in their speech and writing.

The accents and dialects used in spoken English vary from region to region. The grammar we learn first is picked up through our speech, and varies accordingly. However there is, at times, a need for uniformity in our language. If we all follow the same linguistic conventions, communication throughout the English-speaking world is greatly improved. An awareness of this fact helps those children who do not speak Standard English to understand that the way they speak is not wrong, but that it has not been chosen as the standard for the whole country. All children need to learn the standard form of English, as well as appreciating their own dialect.

In their first year of *Jolly Grammar*, the children begin to develop an understanding of how their language works, and are taught some of the accepted grammatical conventions. The teaching in this first year aims to give an elementary understanding of the fact that we speak and write in sentences, and that the words we use fall into categories. These categories are known as parts of speech (they can also be referred to as 'word classes'). The parts of speech introduced in *Jolly Grammar 1* are nouns, pronouns, verbs, adjectives and adverbs. The children also learn how to use verbs to indicate whether something is happening in the past, present or future.

The term 'grammar' is used quite broadly with children of this age. Definitions of the parts of speech, and of what constitutes a sentence, have necessarily been simplified to age-appropriate working definitions. As the children grow older, the definitions can be expanded and refined.

With all teaching there must be a degree of repetition. This is particularly so when teaching a new discipline like grammar. Every lesson should include some revision. Suggestions for revision are provided in the teacher's guidance. However, teachers should feel free to use their own judgement when deciding which areas their children need to revise.

Nouns

A noun denotes a person, place or thing. On the most basic level, nouns can be divided into proper nouns and common nouns.

Proper nouns are essentially names: the name or title of a particular person, place or thing. For example, *John Smith*, *England* and *Mount Everest* are all proper nouns. All nouns that are not specific names or titles are called common nouns.

Common nouns can be further divided into concrete nouns (e.g. *table* or *child*), abstract nouns (e.g. *beauty* or *kindness*) and collective nouns (e.g. the *class* or a *flock* of birds).

> Colour: The colour for nouns is black.

TEACHING IDEAS FOR GRAMMAR

Proper Nouns

The *Jolly Grammar 1 Pupil and Teacher's Books* begin by introducing proper nouns. This is because the children will already be familiar with this kind of noun, albeit indirectly, through their own names. Children like to work with their names, and should already be aware that they start with a capital letter.

The *Jolly Grammar* programme introduces proper nouns as the particular name given to a:

- person, including their surname and title;
- place, for example, a river, mountain, park, street, town, country, continent, planet;
- building, for example, a school, house, library, swimming pool, cinema;
- date, for example, a day of the week, month, religious holiday.

Proper nouns start with a capital letter. When we refer to specific people, places, days and things by their proper names, we use capital letters. For example, we use a capital letter at the beginning of *Anna*, *Lake Victoria* and *Monday*, but not for *girl*, *lake* or *tomorrow*. The capital letters indicate that the name is important. Children can understand that they are themselves important, since they are unique, and that this is why their own name starts with a capital letter.

Action: The action for a proper noun is to touch one's forehead with the index and middle fingers. This is the same action as that used for *name* in British Sign Language.

Colour: The colour for nouns is black.

Common Nouns

Although there are three types of common noun, only concrete nouns are taught in *Jolly Grammar 1*. The intangible nature of abstract nouns, like *happiness*, means that they are difficult for young children to grasp.

Everything we can see has a name by which we can refer to it. The children will enjoy looking around the classroom for examples of objects, such as *table*, *chair*, *desk*, *light*, *carpet*, *ruler* and *pencil*. These names are not specific to any one object, but refer to tables, chairs and so on in general, because of this they are called common nouns and not proper nouns. At this stage, the children find it useful to think of nouns as names for things they can see and touch. A good way to help the children decide if a word is a noun is to encourage them to say *a*, *an* or *the* before the word and see whether it makes sense. For example, *a chair*, *an elephant* and *the table* make sense, whereas *a fell*, *an fluffy* and *the ran* do not.

The words *a*, *an* and *the* are the three articles and are explained later.

In general, children understand the concept of nouns easily, and have no trouble when asked to think of examples. Identifying

Action: The action for a common noun is to touch one's forehead with all the fingers of one hand.

Colour: The colour for nouns is black.

nouns in sentences is more difficult, but comes with practice. In any spare moments, encourage the children to identify the nouns in sentences on the board, or in books.

Plurals

Most nouns change in the plural, that is, when they describe more than one. The *Jolly Grammar 1 Pupil and Teacher's Books* introduce the two regular ways in which a plural can be formed. The simplest way to make a plural is by adding an ‹s› to the end of the noun, as in *dogs*, *cats*, *girls* and *boys*. This way of forming the plural is introduced first. The second way of making the plural applies to those nouns that end with ‹sh›, ‹ch›, ‹s›, ‹z› or ‹x›. These words are usually made plural by adding ‹es›, as in the words *wishes*, *churches*, *kisses* and *foxes*. When children listen carefully, they can hear the different sounds produced by the ‹s› and ‹es› endings. The plural endings ‹s› and ‹es› often sound like /z/ and /iz/, as in *dogs* and *boxes*. Knowing that these words are plurals will help the children to remember to spell the /z/ sound with an ‹s›.

Irregular, or tricky, plurals for example *children*, are not introduced in the *Jolly Grammar 1 Pupil and Teacher's Books*.

Pronouns

Pronouns are the little words used to replace nouns. The *Jolly Grammar 1 Pupil and Teacher's Books* introduce the personal pronouns only. The relative pronouns (e.g. *who*), possessive pronouns (e.g. *mine* and *yours*) and reflexive pronouns (e.g. *myself*) can be taught when the children are older.

Without pronouns, language would become boring and repetitive. To illustrate this in the classroom, give the children an example of a story without pronouns. For example, *Jenny, John and Mary decided to go to the zoo. Jenny, John and Mary prepared some food for a picnic and then Jenny, John and Mary set off…* and so on. By using the pronoun *they*, this kind of repetition can be avoided. Examples of this sort help the children to understand the function of pronouns. The children will also understand why the word *pronoun* has the word *noun* within it, once they recognise that pronouns replace nouns.

There are eight personal pronouns:

I	(first person singular)
you	(second person singular)
he	(third person singular)
she	(third person singular)
it	(third person singular)
we	(first person plural)
you	(second person plural)
they	(third person plural)

Although, in modern English, the word *you* is used for both the second person singular and second person plural pronouns, this is not the case in many languages. In order to make it easier for the children to learn other languages later on, *Jolly Grammar* introduces them to the distinction between *you* used in the singular and *you* used in the plural.

Teaching Ideas for Grammar

Singular pronoun actions:

I   you   he   she   it

I: point to oneself
you: point to someone else
he: point to a boy
she: point to a girl
it: point to the floor

Plural pronoun actions:

we   you   they

we: point in a circle to include self and others
you: point to two other people
they: point to the next-door class

Colour: The colour for pronouns is pink.

Verbs

A verb indicates what a person, or thing, does and can describe an action, an event, a state or a change. It is easiest for children to think of verbs as 'doing words' at first. Ask each child for an example of something they do. Tell the children to put the word *to* before the word, so that they say the verbs in the infinitive form, for example, *to run*, *to hop*, *to sing*, *to play* and so on. This is not something they will find difficult.

Since verbs in English are very complicated, The *Jolly Grammar 1 Pupil and Teacher's Books* introduce only the simple tenses. For instance, in the case of the verb root *cook*, the infinitive is *to cook*, the simple present tense is *cook*, the simple past tense is *cooked*, and the simple future is *will cook*. Later, when the children learn the continuous and perfect modes of the verb, they can be told that the verbs they first learnt were known as the simple tenses. For reference, the table below shows all three modes in past, present and future:

	Past	Present	Future
Simple	*looked*	*look*	*will look*
Continuous	*was looking*	*is looking*	*will be looking*
Perfect	*had looked*	*have looked*	*will have looked*

Technically, there is no future tense in English. This is because, unlike the past tense, the future is not formed by modifying the verb root itself. However, at this stage it is helpful for the children to think of verbs as taking place in the past, present and future. The various complexities can be taught when the children are older.

Action: The action for verbs is to clench fists and move arms backwards and forwards at one's sides, as if running.

Colour: The colour for verbs is red.

Conjugating verbs: the present

Even at this early stage, the children can learn how to conjugate regular verbs. This means saying the pronouns in order, with the correct form of the verb after each one. Understanding what it means to conjugate a verb will not only benefit the children's literacy skills, but will also help them when they come to learn other languages later on. A good way to introduce this exercise is by demonstrating how to conjugate the verb *to run* in the present tense, and by doing the appropriate pronoun actions:

> I run
> you run
> he runs
> she runs
> it runs
> we run
> you run
> they run

Encourage the children to notice how the verb changes after *he*, *she* and *it*. With regular verbs, an ‹s› is added to the verb root after these pronouns; this is called the third person singular marker.

Action: The action for the present tense is pointing towards the floor with the palm of the hand.

Colour: The colour for verbs is red.

Conjugating verbs: the past

The children need to have an understanding of what the past is. Initially, it can be helpful for them to think in terms of what happened yesterday; for example, *Yesterday I jumped*.

The regular past tense is formed by adding the suffix ‹-ed› to the root of the verb. When introducing the past tense, it is best to choose a regular verb to work with rather than asking the children for suggestions, as many verbs have a 'tricky' or irregular past form. Good examples verbs with regular past tenses are: *to jump* (*jumped*), *to cook* (*cooked*) and *to play* (*played*). It is helpful to demonstrate (with the appropriate pronoun actions) how to conjugate a regular verb in the past tense:

> I cooked
> you cooked
> he cooked
> she cooked
> it cooked
> we cooked
> you cooked
> they cooked

Write this conjugation on the board, so that the children can see which letters have been added to the verb root in each case. In this way, they can discover for themselves that, in this case, the suffix ‹-ed› is always added to the root. If the verb root ends with an ‹e›, as in the word *bake*, the ‹e› must be removed before the ‹-ed› suffix is added. The ‹-ed› ending can be pronounced in one of three ways: /t/, as in *slipped*, /d/, as in *smiled* or /id/, as in *waited*.

> Action: The action for the past tense is pointing backwards over one's shoulder with a thumb.
>
> Colour: The colour for verbs is red.

Generally, if a verb has a short vowel sound, there should be two consonants between the short vowel and the ‹-ed› suffix. If there is only one consonant after the short vowel, this letter is doubled before the suffix is added. The list, below left, shows some examples of the verbs to which this doubling rule applies. The list, below right, shows some verbs to which the doubling rule does not apply.

Doubling rule applies to:		Doubling rule does not apply to:	
bat	→ batted	pick	→ picked
hop	→ hopped	hand	→ handed
pin	→ pinned	rest	→ rested
rip	→ ripped	lift	→ lifted
hug	→ hugged	wish	→ wished
trap	→ trapped	shift	→ shifted

Gradually, the children will learn to apply this useful doubling rule.

Although at first only verbs with regular past tenses are introduced, it is not long before the children realise that some verbs have 'tricky' past tenses. They may want to conjugate a verb of their own choosing, such as *to run*. It is interesting to see how quickly some of the children realise that the past tense is not 'I runned, you runned', but *I ran*, *you ran*, and so on. Those children who are in the habit of regularising the past tense of irregular verbs in their speech (by saying 'I runned', for example) will have to learn the standard irregular forms.

Conjugating verbs: the future

Just as the word *yesterday* was used to help the children achieve an idea of the past, the children learn to understand what the future is by thinking in terms of *tomorrow*; for example, *Tomorrow, I shall post my letter*.

With simple verbs, when we speak of the future we use verb root with the auxiliary verbs *will*,

> Action: The action for verbs that describe the future is pointing towards the front.
>
> Colour: The colour for verbs is red.

Teaching Ideas for Grammar

or *shall*, in front of it. The auxiliary verb *will* can be used with all the pronouns, but *shall* should only be used with *I* or *we* (the first person singular or the first person plural). Demonstrate how to conjugate a regular verb in the future, doing the pronoun actions:

I shall swim
you will swim
he will swim
she will swim
it will swim
we shall swim
you will swim
they will swim

Adjectives

An adjective is a word that describes a noun or a pronoun. At first, it is sufficient to tell the children that an adjective describes a noun. Start by asking the class to think of a noun, for example, *a cat*. Ask one child for a word to describe the cat, and say the words together, for example, *a black cat*. Then ask another child for a second adjective and add it into the phrase, for example, *a noisy black cat*. After several examples, the children will begin to understand how an adjective functions, especially when used directly before a noun.

When the children begin to apply their knowledge of adjectives to their work, their writing will become more interesting. Adjectives help the reader to imagine what is being described.

Action: The action for an adjective is to touch the side of the temple with one's fist.

Colour: The colour for adjectives is blue.

Adverbs

An adverb is similar to an adjective, in that they are both describing words. However, an adverb describes a verb rather than a noun. Usually adverbs describe how, where, when or how often something happens. They can also be used to modify adjectives or other adverbs, but the children do not need to know that at this stage.

Start by asking the class to think of a verb, for example, *to swim*. Ask one child for a word to describe this verb, and say the words together, for example, *to swim slowly*. (When the verb is in the infinitive form, as in this case, the adverb should come after the root *swim*, in order to avoid creating a split infinitive. A split infinitive occurs when an adverb is placed between the two parts of the infinitive form of the verb, splitting it up, as in *to slowly swim*, or *to boldly go*.) After several examples, the children

Action: The action for an adverb is to bang one fist on top of the other.

Colour: The colour for adverbs is orange.

begin to understand how an adverb functions. At this stage, it helps if the children think of an adverb as being found next to a verb, and recognise adverbs by the fact that they often end with the suffix ‹-ly›. However, the children will soon discover many instances where this is not the case and they will need to refine their understanding.

Definite and indefinite articles: the, a, an

The words *a*, *an* and *the* are known as articles. *A* and *an* are used before singular nouns and are called the indefinite articles, as in *a man* and *an egg*. *The* is used before singular and plural nouns and is called the definite article, as in *the dog* and *the boys*. The articles are a special sort of adjective.

Individual schools can decide whether or not they use the full terminology at this stage. Whilst young children like learning new and difficult words, there is a limit to how many they can cope with at once. For most children it is sufficient to refer to these words as 'articles'.

Children need to learn when to use *an* instead of *a*. As a simple rule of thumb, tell them to look at the noun that comes after the article. If the first letter is a vowel, then they should use *an*, as with *an apple*, *an egg*, *an itch*, *an orange*, *an umbrella*. However, there are some exceptions to this rule, which the children may notice. If a word starts with a long u sound, as in *unicorn* and *union*, the correct article is *a*. This is because the long u sound is in fact made up of two sounds, the first of which is the consonant /y/. The same reasoning can be applied to words that start with a silent ‹h›. Since the consonant ‹h› is silent, the first sound that is actually heard is a vowel, so these words take the article *an*, for example, *an hour, an heir*.

Sentences

It is difficult to define a sentence in a way that can be readily understood by small children. However, because the children speak in sentences, they already have a general sense of a sentence as expressing a complete thought. If each child is asked to say one sentence of news about their weekend, the majority will be able to do this.

At this stage, it is sufficient for the children to know that a sentence starts with a capital letter, ends with a full stop, and must make sense. Soon, they will learn that a sentence must also have a verb, and eventually that it must have a subject too. Although the children are not ready to learn the full definition at this stage, it is still important that they learn about sentences. This knowledge helps them to organise their writing into manageable units, and avoid linking one idea after another with the word *and*.

Questions

The children need to understand what a question is and how to form a question mark correctly. If a sentence is worded in such a way that it expects an answer, then it is a question and needs to be followed by a question mark instead of a full stop. The children need to practise many examples before they are able to remember this automatically. It can be helpful if the teacher encourages the children to spot spoken questions. For example, the teacher can say a number of sentences and encourage the children to indicate whether each sentence is a question or not. Once this exercise becomes familiar the roles can be reversed, and the children can try to think up the sentences.

Parsing: identifying parts of speech in sentences

Parsing means identifying the function, or part of speech, of each word in a sentence. The children must look at each word in context to decide which part of speech it is. For example, the sentence *Six boys swam quickly.* can be parsed as: adjective (*six*), common noun (*boys*), verb (*swam*), adverb (*quickly*).

Many words can function as more than one part of speech; for example, the word *light* can be a noun (*the light*), a verb (*to light*), or an adjective (*the light colour*). It is only by analysing a word's use within a sentence that its function can be identified.

The children's ability to parse will develop gradually with regular practice. There are different ways to practise parsing. Start by writing simple sentences on the board and encourage the children to identify the parts of speech. First ask the class (or select one child) to read the sentence. Then point to one of the words and ask the children to call out which part of speech it is, or to do the appropriate action. Alternatively, ask individual children to come to the board, pick a word, and underline it in the appropriate colour for that part of speech. Another classroom activity involves doing the action for one part of speech, and choosing a child to find an example of it in the sentence. The child can then underline the part of speech in the appropriate colour. Alternatively, have the class copy down the sentence and underline each part of speech in the appropriate colour.

Improving vocabulary and using a dictionary

The speed at which children acquire vocabulary varies enormously. Many children do not find it easy to learn new words. They have to hear a word a great many times before adopting it into their own vocabulary.

We all use far fewer words in normal speech than we encounter in writing. It follows, then, that the more a child reads, the greater the likelihood of their vocabulary increasing. However, private reading alone is too haphazard a method to rely upon. This is especially true for those children who do not have someone at home who is willing and able to explain the meanings of unfamiliar words.

If a new word is introduced and defined for the children in the classroom, very few are able to recall it or say what it means the following day. To learn a word properly, most children will need to encounter it on several different occasions. They will also need to practise saying the word, and using it in their own spoken sentences. A systematic approach to vocabulary teaching is therefore very important.

The *Jolly Grammar 1 Pupil and Teacher's Books* introduce many words that will be unfamiliar to the children. Obviously, the grammatical terms themselves will be new to the children, and possibly some of the words in the spelling lists will be new too. It is a good idea to choose a selection of new words and teach them systematically to the children. Teachers should select words that are appropriate for their particular class, and should use enough repetition to ensure that the words are mastered.

Teaching Ideas for Grammar

Young children, who are able to read and to decode new words, are fascinated by dictionaries. Once they are familiar with the alphabet and understand how the dictionary works, they enjoy finding words for themselves. Most children are capable of learning to use a dictionary that has been designed for use in schools. Reading the meanings of the words that they find helps to improve the children's comprehension skills. This is a good habit, which should be encouraged. The frequent practice of alphabet and dictionary work in the *Jolly Grammar 1 Pupil Book* is designed to help the children acquire good dictionary skills.

The *Jolly Dictionary* is an important part of the Jolly Grammar programme. Throughout the *Jolly Grammar* and *Jolly Phonics* programmes, the children are taught to recite the alphabet in four groups: A-E, F-M, N-S, and T-Z. The letter groups are colour coded and are introduced with their associated colours in the Jolly Learning products, as seen here in the *Alphabet Poster*.

By learning the alphabet in this way, the children are better prepared for using the *Jolly Dictionary*, which is similarly divided up into four colour-coded sections. Each of the sections contains about a quarter of the words in the dictionary. The corresponding colour-coded page edges help the children to locate words quickly and easily. When the children have found the word they are looking for, the clear pronunciation guides show them how to say the words correctly.

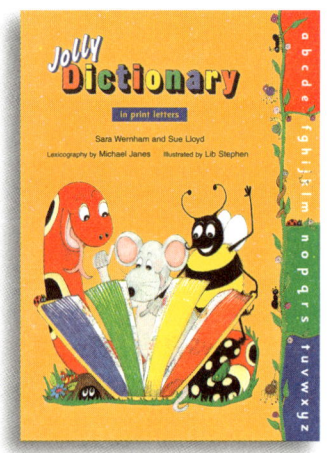

When children first begin to write independently, their efforts should be encouraged regardless of the quality of their writing. However, after a year of writing freely, the children are ready to learn how they can improve their written work. The *Jolly Grammar 1 Pupil Book* encourages the children to think of alternatives for words they commonly overuse, like *said*.

Teaching ideas for spelling

Most children need to be taught to spell correctly. In *Jolly Grammar*, spelling is the main focus for one of the two weekly lessons.

There are a few children who learn to spell well through their reading. These children have a good memory for words. They teach themselves the code of English, mentally noting the different ways that the sounds are represented as they read. When these children come to write, they use analogy to work out how to spell unfamiliar words. Even when they are unsure of a spelling, these children are often able to work it out, by writing the word in several ways and choosing the correct version. It does not necessarily follow that these children are more intelligent, or produce superior writing. It simply means that they have the necessary combination of attributes for accurate spelling, namely an excellent retentive memory for print, good phonological awareness and strong reasoning skills. When these children are taught the alphabetic code explicitly, they learn even faster.

Just as there are a few children who find it easy to spell accurately, there are some who find it exceedingly difficult. These children often have spatial problems, a poor auditory/visual memory, or are inclined to muddle the sequence and direction of letters in words. It is important to identify a child's individual difficulty, because whatever the problem, it has to be overcome. These children need a good grasp of phonics, and must recognise that they need to work harder and with more self-discipline, if they are to achieve satisfactory results. Parental help is especially important for these children.

Most children taught with *Jolly Phonics* in their first year at school will be familiar with the vowel digraphs and the alternative ways of spelling the vowel sounds. However, this does not mean that they will know all the alternative spellings by heart. The aim of the spelling work in the *Jolly Grammar 1 Pupil Book* is to reinforce the teaching that has gone before, and to extend the children's phonic knowledge.

In the *Jolly Phonics Pupil Books*, the children were taught to spell a word by listening for all the sounds in that word and writing the sounds in the correct order. This remains the default spelling method in the *Jolly Grammar 1 Pupil Book*. The children are given the opportunity to practise using this spelling technique in their weekly spelling tests. To further improve the accuracy of the children's spelling, the *Jolly Grammar 1 Pupil Book* also teaches the following spelling features:

1. Vowel digraphs

2. Alternative spellings of vowel sounds

3. Plural endings

4. Short vowels and consonant doubling

5. Tricky words

6. Consonant blends

These six features are outlined in greater detail in the following pages.

1. Vowel digraphs

The children should already be familiar with the blending technique: 'If the short vowel sound doesn't work, try the long vowel'. For example, when the children are reading words with an ‹i› spelling, such as *life*, *mind* and *pipe*, if the /i/ sound, in *sit*, does not make sense, they should try the /ie/ sound, as in *pie*. The children can use the same technique with the other four vowels as well, and this enables them to decode many unfamiliar words. However, this technique is only useful for reading, and will not help the children in their writing. If they are to spell accurately, the children need a more thorough understanding of how the vowels work.

Vowel digraph is the term used for two letters that make a single vowel sound. At least one of these letters is always a vowel. Often the two letters are placed next to each other in a word. For example, the ‹a› and ‹y› that make up the ‹ay› digraph in *hay* are adjacent, likewise the ‹ea› in *tea*, the ‹ou› in *out*, the ‹oi› in *oil*, and the ‹ew› in *few*. Two vowel letters are usually needed to make a long vowel sound. The long vowel sounds are the same as the names of the vowel letters: /ai/, /ee/, /ie/, /oa/ or /ue/. Generally, the sound made by a vowel digraph is that of the first vowel's name. Hence the well-known rule of thumb 'When two vowels go walking, the first does the talking'.

Sometimes, the long vowel sound is made by two vowels separated by a consonant. In monosyllabic words, the second vowel is usually an ‹e›, known as a 'magic ‹e›' because it modifies the sound of the first vowel. Digraphs with a magic ‹e› can be thought of as 'hop-over ‹e›' digraphs; examples are: ‹a_e›, ‹e_e›, ‹i_e›, ‹o_e› and ‹u_e›. Once again, the sound they make is that of the first vowel's name; the magic ‹e› is silent. Children like to show with their hands how the magic from the ‹e› hops over the preceding consonant and changes the short vowel sound to a long one.

The hop-over ‹e› digraphs are an alternative way of making the long vowel sounds, and are found in such words as *bake*, *these*, *fine*, *hope* and *cube*. The children need to be shown many examples of words with hop-over ‹e› digraphs. It is possible to illustrate the function of the magic ‹e› in such words, by using a piece of paper to cover the ‹e› and reading the word first with the magic ‹e›, and then without it. For example, *pipe* becomes *pip* without the magic ‹e›; *hate* becomes *hat*; *hope* becomes *hop* and *late* becomes *lat*. The children may like to try this themselves. It does not matter if, as in the *late-lat* example, they find themselves producing nonsense words. The exercise will still help them to understand the spelling rule. When looking at text on the board or in big books, children can be encouraged to look for and identify words with a magic ‹e›.

Although hop-over ‹e› words are generally quite common, there are only a limited number of words with the ‹e_e› spelling; examples include *these*, *scheme* and *complete*. Such words are not only rather rare, but are also found most often in complicated words. For this reason, the ‹e_e› spelling is not given as much emphasis as the other the long vowel spellings. However, it is worth introducing it to the class.

2. Alternative spellings of vowel sounds

The complicated aspects of English spelling should be made so familiar to the children as to become automatic. For example, if the children read *The brave man stayed on the train*, they should be able to identify all the /ai/ sounds in the words: the ‹a_e› in *brave*, the ‹ay› in *stayed*, and the ‹ai› in *train*. By looking out for this kind of spelling feature in text on the board and in books on a regular basis, the children will soon learn to apply their knowledge in their reading and writing. It is important that all children acquire these skills. For this reason, the alternative letter sound spellings should be revised regularly with flash cards.

In the *Jolly Grammar 1 Pupil Book*, the main focus is on the vowel sounds and their alternative spellings. The list below shows the first spelling taught for each letter sound and the main alternatives that are introduced:

First spelling taught:	Alternative spellings for sound:	Examples of all spellings in words:
‹ai›	‹ay›, ‹a_e›	rain, day, came
‹ee›	‹ea›	street, dream
‹ie›	‹igh›, ‹y›, ‹i_e›	pie, light, by, time
‹oa›	‹ow›, ‹o_e›	boat, snow, home
‹ue›	‹ew›, ‹u_e›	due, few, cube
‹er›	‹ir›, ‹ur›	her, first, turn
‹oi›	‹oy›	boil, toy
‹ou›	‹ow›	out, cow
‹or›	‹au›, ‹aw›, ‹al›	corn, sauce, saw, talk

3. Plural endings

Plurals are introduced to the children in the grammar lessons. However, there is a direct spin-off into spelling. By recognising when a word is plural, children can avoid making errors like spelling *ducks* as 'dux'. Likewise, knowing that words ending in ‹sh›, ‹ch›, ‹x›, ‹s› and ‹z› are made plural with the addition of an ‹es› suffix, also helps the children to spell accurately.

4. Short vowels and consonant doubling

There are always some exceptions to a rule. This saying is also true of spelling rules in English. It will almost always be possible to find a few words that contradict a particular spelling rule. That said, most rules are pretty reliable, and they make the spelling patterns much easier for the children to learn. One such rule is the doubling rule. Hundreds of words follow this rule and very few do not, so it is definitely worth teaching.

The rule of consonant doubling is governed by the short vowels, so the children need to be able to identify the short vowel sounds confidently. An entertaining way to encourage the children to listen for short vowels involves a puppet and a box, and is as follows:

For /**a**/, the teacher says the /a/ sound and puts the puppet **a**t the side of the box.
For /**e**/, the teacher says the /e/ sound and makes the puppet wobble on the **e**dge of the box.
For /**i**/, the teacher says the /i/ sound and puts the puppet **i**n the box.
For /**o**/, the teacher says the /o/ sound and puts the puppet **o**n top of the box.
For /**u**/, the teacher says the /u/ sound and puts the puppet **u**nderneath the box.

Then the children can pretend that their fist is the box and their hand is the puppet.

Start by calling out the short vowel sounds. For each one, the children do the appropriate action with their hands. Then call out short words that contain a short vowel; good examples include *pot*, *hat*, *bun*, *dig*, *red*. The children should listen for the vowel sound in each word, and do the action. When most of the children have mastered this, progress to calling out short words with a variety of vowel sounds. For those words that do not have a short vowel sound, the children must keep their hands still.

Activities like these help to keep the children 'tuned in' to identifying the sounds in words, as well as preparing them for the following rules:

Rules for consonant doubling:

a. In a short (i.e. monosyllabic) word with a short vowel sound, ending in /f/, /l/, /s/ or /z/, the final consonant is doubled, as in the words *cliff*, *bell*, *miss*, and *buzz*.

b. In a short word with a short vowel sound, if the last consonant sound is /k/, this is spelt as ‹ck›, as in the words *back*, *neck*, *lick*, *clock*, *duck*.

c. If there is only one consonant after a short, stressed vowel sound, this consonant is doubled before any suffix starting with a vowel is added. For example, when the suffixes ‹-ed›, ‹-er›, ‹-est›, ‹-ing› and ‹-y› are added to the words *hop*, *wet*, *big*, *clap* and *fun*, the final consonants are doubled so that we get *hopped*, *wetter*, *biggest*, *clapping* and *funny*. Note that when ‹y› is a suffix, it counts as a vowel because it has a vowel sound. (This rule does not apply to those words where the final consonant is ‹x›, because ‹x› is really the two consonant sounds /k/ and /s/. This means that the ‹x› is never doubled, even in words like *faxed*, *boxing* and *mixer*.)

Where the suffixes begin with the letter ‹e›, it can help the children to think of the two consonants as forming a wall between the short vowel and the ‹e›. If there were only one consonant, the wall would not be thick enough to prevent 'magic' hopping over from the ‹e›, and changing the short vowel sound into a long one. With two consonants, the wall becomes so thick that the 'magic' cannot get over it.

d. When a word ends with the letters ‹le›, and the preceding syllable contains a short, stressed vowel sound, there must be two consonants between the short vowel and the ‹le›. This means that the consonant before the ‹le› is doubled in words like *paddle*, *kettle*, *nibble*, *topple* and *snuggle*. No doubling is necessary in words like *handle*, *twinkle* and *jungle* because they already have two consonants between the short vowel and the ‹le›.

Young children tend not to grasp these spelling rules straight away, but learn them easily if the rules are regularly brought to their attention. As with many skills, success is dependent upon constant repetition.

5. Tricky Words

The tricky words are a group of frequently used words, which the children need to learn by heart. Most of the tricky words have irregular spellings. The few tricky words that are phonically regular are referred to as tricky words because they are introduced before the alternative letter sound spellings they contain have been taught. The children will need to memorise the 'tricky parts' of each word for reading and spelling. The seventy-two tricky words introduced in *Jolly Phonics Pupil Books 1, 2* and *3* are revised in the *Jolly Grammar 1 Pupil Book*. Each weekly spelling list includes two tricky words. The complete list of all seventy-two words is listed on the following page.

Teaching Ideas for Spelling

The seventy-two tricky words revised in the *Jolly Grammar 1 Pupil Book* are:

Look, copy, cover, write, check

The children can practise spelling the tricky words using the 'Look, copy, cover, write check' method. This was the principal method used for teaching the tricky words in the *Jolly Phonics Pupil Books*.

For this activity, the children will need some lined paper, which has been divided up into four columns. In the first column, the children write out the tricky word(s) they are practising. The children look at the first word and identify the tricky part(s). For instance, the word *said* has an /e/ sound in the middle, but it is spelt with an ‹ai›. The ‹s› and ‹d› are regular. Then the children say the letter names (not the letter sounds) several times. The reason for saying the names rather than the sounds is that the letter names trot off the tongue more easily and these particular words do not sound out reliably. After that, the children trace the word in the air or on the table, saying the letter names as they do so.

Following that, they copy the word into the second column, saying the letter names again. Then they cover up the word, and write it on their own in the third column, looking back to see if it is correct. This is repeated in the last column. Encourage the children to continue saying the letter names as they write the word. Regular revision and dictation ensure that the spelling of these words is mastered.

6. Consonant blends

It is worth devoting some time to practising the consonant blends. Revision of initial and final consonant blends is provided in the grammar lessons, and each of the weekly spelling lists includes a regular word with a different consonant blend.

The children will read unfamiliar words with greater ease once they can blend consonants together fluently, instead of sounding out each consonant on its own. For example, the children should aim to say '/dr/-/u/-/m/', and not '/d/-/r/-/u/-/m/' when blending *drum*. Flash cards showing the consonant blends can be used for regular blending practice. For writing, however, the children need to be aware of the individual sounds in a consonant blend. Often, children will write a word such as *drum* as 'dum', because they do not hear the second sound in the blend. This problem can be overcome with regular practice. Call out consonant blends and ask the children to say the individual sounds, holding up a finger for each sound as they say it. For example, when the children hear /dr/, they should say /d/, /r/ showing two fingers, and when they hear /scr/ they should say /s/, /c/, /r/, showing three fingers.

Improving spelling through phonic knowledge

Simply copying words does surprisingly little to improve the children's spelling. For instance, some children will write the day of the week on all their work by copying from the board or from a wall chart. Yet, even after years of doing so on a daily basis, many will still be unable to spell these words without copying. However, if such words are taught thoroughly and are practised without copying, these same children will be quite capable of learning how to spell them. When teaching the spelling of words, like the days of the week, it is helpful first to analyse each word to see how it is made up. Appropriate spelling techniques can then be chosen to help the children memorise the irregular elements in each word. For example, helpful spelling techniques for teaching the days of the week are as follows:

> *Monday*
> Encourage the children to use the 'say it as it sounds' technique when spelling this word; emphasise the short /o/, so that the ‹Mon› of *Monday* rhymes with *gone*.
>
> *Tuesday*
> The children listen for, and say, the sounds /T/-/ue/-/z/-/d/-/ai/. They should be familiar with the ‹ay› spelling of the /ai/ sound, which comes at the end of this word, and the fact that ‹s› is sometimes pronounced /z/, as it is in *Tuesday*. However, the children may need reminding about the ‹ue›; ask them repeatedly how the /ue/ sound is spelt in *Tuesday*.

Wednesday
Use the 'say it as it sounds' technique when teaching this word. Split *Wednesday* up into its separate syllables, 'Wed-nes-day', and stress the usually swallowed sounds.

Thursday
The children listen for, and say, the sounds /Th/-/er/-/z/-/d/-/ai/. Ask them repeatedly how the /er/ sound is spelt in *Thursday*.

Friday
Use the 'say it as it sounds' technique, pronouncing the word with a short /i/ sound so that the ‹Frid› of *Friday* rhymes with *rid*.

Saturday
Split this word up into its separate syllables, 'Sat-ur-day'. Ask the children repeatedly how the /er/ sound is spelt in *Saturday*.

Sunday
This is the only day of the week with a perfectly predictable spelling.

Once the days of the week have been taught thoroughly, teachers can write the date on the board using the initial letters only to indicate the day of the week. This encourages the children to practise the spellings they have learnt. In spare moments when looking at books with the children, it helps to look closely at the spellings of some of the words. This helps to develop the children's ability to apply their phonic knowledge to spelling. For example, if the word *circus* appears in the text, teachers can ask the children why the first ‹c› has a /s/ sound, or which spelling of the /er/ sound is being used. Teachers can also point out that pronouncing the last syllable, ‹us›, as it sounds makes the spelling easier to remember. After a while, this kind of analytic thinking becomes second nature to the children.

Spelling and Grammar Lessons

For each lesson there is an activity page in the *Pupil Book* for the children to complete and an accompanying page of teaching guidance in the *Teacher's Book*. The recommendations in the teacher's guidance are intended to be followed systematically. However, if a suggestion seems inappropriate for a particular class situation, it can of course be adapted to suit.

Each page of teacher's guidance also features a reduced copy of the relevant activity page in the *Pupil Book*. It can be helpful to refer to this prior to, or during, the lesson.

Spelling lessons

The spelling lessons all follow the same basic format:

    a. Spelling Test

    b. Revision

    c. Letter Sound

    d. Spelling List

    e. Activity Page

    f. Dictation

The list of words and sentences for dictation and the weekly spelling list are provided in the teacher's guidance.

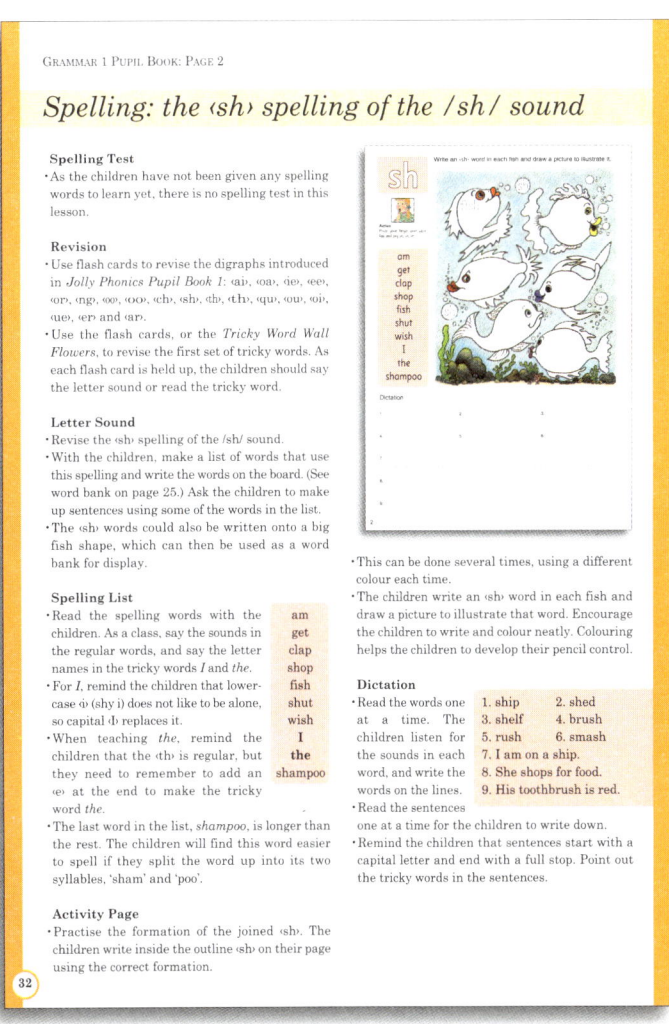

Many teaching points are common to all the spelling lessons, so these are explained in further detail on the following pages.

a. Spelling Test

Six pages have been provided at the back of the *Jolly Grammar 1 Pupil Book* for the children's spelling tests (pages 74 to 79).

Start by telling the children to turn to the back of their books and find the space for that particular week's spelling test. Call out the words one at a time for the children to write on the lines. Repeat each word twice, giving the children just enough time to write the word before moving on to the next one. The words can be called out in the same order as they appear in the list, but it is best if they are called out in a random order. Those children who are finding it difficult can be given fewer words to learn.

b. Revision

Each lesson should start with a short burst of flash card revision. To begin with, teachers should concentrate on revising the letter sounds that have already been taught, particularly the digraphs. After the first six weeks or so, drop the digraphs that the children know well and concentrate on those they are unsure of. Add each alternative spelling to the revision session as it is taught. After week seven, add the single vowel letters /a/, /e/, /i/, /o/, and /u/. Make sure that the children are aware of both the short vowel sounds (usually made by a single letter) and the long vowel sounds (usually made by a digraph). Over the course of the year, other areas can be added to the revision session. Useful examples include consonant blends, identifying sounds in words, reciting the alphabet, and calling out the letter names tricky words.

c. Letter Sound

The main focus of the majority of the spelling lessons is a digraph, with one being featured each week. Begin by helping the children to compile a list of words that contain the letter-sound spelling being taught. These words can then be written on the board for the children to sound out and blend. It is a good idea to prepare a list of regular words using each of the digraphs for this purpose. The table opposite provides a small number of suitable words, which can be used as a starting point. Encourage the children to make up sentences using some of the words on the board. Children are more likely to remember new words if they are given the opportunity to practise using them.

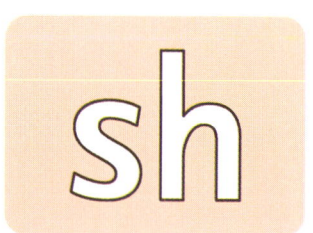

Spelling and Grammar Lessons

Pupil Book page:	Spelling pattern:	Word bank:
2	‹sh›	shelf, dish, ship, shop, brush, shed, dash, rash, shell, starfish, splashing, mushroom
4	‹ch›	chin, chess, bench, check, chimp, lunch, coach, cheek, torch, pinch, chilling, drench
6	‹th› as /th/ and /th/	them, slither, smooth, with, then, than; moth, thorn, three, cloth, toothbrush, froth, teeth
8	‹ng›	strength, wing, sang, prong, string, stung; swings, ping-pong, longer, length, dangling, flung
10	‹qu›	quilt, quest, liquid, quit, quiz, quill, squid, squirrel, quail, queen, quack, quench
12	‹ar›	park, march, shark, barn, mark, jar, dart, charming, scarf, farmer, cartoon, smartest
14	**Short Vowels**	bag, cap, pat, rag, hat, rat; net, pen, leg, men, pet, gem; bin, tip, bib zip, fig, pit; box, top, dog, pot, hop, rod; mug, cup, rug, mud, bun, dug, fun
16	‹ff›	staff, fluff, stuffing, cuff, toffee, coffee, muffin, puff, gruff, huff, chaffinch, scruffy, riff, cliff, handcuffs
18	‹ll›	well, hill, smell, seagull, jelly, drill, doll, yelling, silly, fell, collar, anthill
20	‹ss› and ‹zz›	messy, press, cress, moss, class, floss, glossy, cross, actress, hissing; fizzy, dizzy
22	‹ck›	chicken, sack, bricks, deck, lock, duck, back, socks, rocking, crackers, cockroach, tracks
24	‹y› as /ee/	party, ferry, sunny, puppy, daisy, berry, army, marry, happy, thirty, muddy, hilly
28	‹a_e›	gave, save, tale, wave, slate, cave, agate, late, shapes, rake, bake, fade
30	‹i_e›	pride, stripe, side, like, life, pipe, quite, bite, wife, nine, fine, fire
32	‹o_e›	closed, slope, alone, drove, broke, hope, choke, globe, zone, joke, note, froze
34	‹u_e› as /ue/ and /oo/	use, muse, fuse, mute, cute, refuse; exclude, flute, rude, prune, rule, plume
36	‹wh›	whiskers, why, whip, while, whisk, whimper, wheat, white, when, wheelbarrow, whisper, which

Spelling and Grammar Lessons

Pupil Book page:	Spelling pattern:	Word bank:
38	⟨ay⟩ as /ai/	*spray, playing, stray, daytime, staying, tray, haystack, pay, runway, yesterday, bay, clay*
40	⟨ea⟩ as /ee/	*peanut, peach, teacher, cream, beak, cleanest, seal, pea, leaf, heat, team, sheaf*
42	⟨igh⟩ as /ie/	*midnight, lighter, sigh, thigh, sight, brightest, tight, right, frighten, slight, high, flight*
44	⟨y⟩ as /ie/	*python, flying, try, satisfy, nylon, pry, sky, rely, apply, myself, spy, cry*
46	⟨ow⟩ as /oa/	*mowing, pillow, lowest, marrow, window, shadow, slow, glowing, flow, rowing, own, arrow*
48	⟨ew⟩ as /ue/ and /oo/	*skew, newt, few, news, stew, dew; jewels, grew, blew, drew, flew, threw,*
50	⟨ou⟩	*cloud, sprout, shouting, spout, proud, ground, pouch, trout, loudest, pound, flour, count*
52	⟨ow⟩ as /ou/	*town, cow, powder, flowers, crown, gown, owls, clown, tower, down, towel, vowel*
54	⟨oi⟩	*moist, ointment, soil, foil, pointing, coil, join, boiling, joint, coins, spoil, toil*
56	⟨oy⟩ as /oi/	*boys, destroying, employ, annoying, royal, ahoy, enjoys, boyish, alloy, oyster, loyal, toyshop, joy*
58	⟨or⟩	*corn, torch, sport, story, horn, fort, fork, north, forty, stormy, snort, morning*
60	⟨al⟩ as /or/	*ball, wall, tallest, falling, chalk, hall, smallest, calling, chalky, talking, stalk, all*
62	⟨nk⟩ as /ng-k/	*trunk, winking, rink, link, plank, tank, Inky, pink, bank, bunk, thinks, twinkling*
64	⟨er⟩	*fern, silver, slippers, herb, letters, blister, butter, river, herd, winter, supper, perch*
66	⟨ir⟩ as /er/	*blackbird, fir, thirsty, thirteen, stir, twirling, birthday, first, swirl, skirt, dirty, chirp*
68	⟨ur⟩ as /er/	*curly, purring, furry, turnip, purse, turf, burglar, further, burst, burning, turn, hurt*
70	⟨au⟩ as /or/	*author, launch, taunt, haunted, laundry, cause, astronaut, August, haunt, haul, pausing, causing*
72	⟨aw⟩ as /or/	*lawn, sawdust, hawk, crawl, dawn, paws, jaw, claw, raw, shawl, trawler, strawberry, yawn, draw, law*

d. Spelling List

Each week the children are given ten spellings to learn for a test. It is a good idea to give the spelling homework at the beginning of the week and to test the children at the end of the week, or on the following Monday.

The spelling words have been carefully selected to enable every child to have some success, with the majority achieving full marks. Words one and two in each spelling list are regular two- or three-letter words and the third word is also regular, but with a consonant blend. All the children should be able to spell these words correctly by listening for the sounds. Words four, five, six, seven and ten generally feature the spelling of the week, and are usually regular. The tenth spelling is usually a longer, more challenging word. The children need encouragement in tackling longer words to build their confidence. Words eight and nine are tricky words; these words need to be practised. The children can learn these words by repeating the letter names, and by using the 'Look, Copy, Cover, Write, Check' method, outlined on pages 20 and 21. Allow a few minutes each day for reciting the letter names of these two words, especially with those children who normally fail to get full marks in their spelling tests. It is important to go over the words on the list during the spelling lesson. It is not enough simply to send home a list of words for the children to learn.

1. am
2. get
3. clap
4. shop
5. fish
6. shut
7. wish
8. I
9. the
10. shampoo

Begin by reading the spelling words with the children. Say the sounds in the regular words (words one to seven, and ten), then blend the sounds together. For example, say '/w/, /i/, /sh/, *wish*'. Say the letter names in the tricky words (words eight and nine) and point out the tricky element(s) in the word. For example, when teaching *the*, remind the children that the ‹th› is regular, but they need to remember to add an ‹e› at the end to make the tricky word *the*. Next, say the regular words again and ask the children to respond with the component sounds. Encourage the children to count the sounds on their fingers. At odd moments during the week ask some of the children to spell, or sound out, a few words from the list, or to test each other in pairs.

Each child takes the list of spellings home to learn. If the children usually leave their *Pupil Books* at school, the words can be written in a small homework book for the children to take home.

Test and mark the spellings each week. The results can be written in the children's *Pupil Book*, or in their homework book, for the parents to see. The marks can be shown either as a score out of ten, or with a coded system if preferred. For example, a coloured star system might be used, with a gold star for 10/10, a silver star for 9/10 and a coloured star for 8/10. Most parents like to be involved in their children's homework and are interested in how many words their child spelt correctly, and which words were mis-spelt.

The children need to be aware that accurate spelling is important. Unfortunately, there is no magic wand that can be waved to make them good at spelling; a certain amount of dedication and practice is needed.

SPELLING AND GRAMMAR LESSONS

In *Jolly Phonics* the children were introduced to three spelling techniques:

    a. 'Look, Copy, Cover, Write, Check',
    b. 'Say as it sounds',
    c. Mnemonics.

Teachers should continue to encourage the children to use these spelling techniques throughout *Jolly Grammar 1*.

e. Activity Page

The picture on each *Pupil Book* page reflects the main teaching point of that week's spelling lesson, whether it is a digraph, a trigraph, or the short vowels.

Encourage the children to think of lots of different words containing the spelling pattern of the week. They may need some help with this. Write all the words on the board. (The words could also be noted down and turned into a class word bank, which builds up week by week.) The children then choose a word to write in each shape, or fill in the missing letters in the words provided, and draw a picture to illustrate each word.

Always encourage the children to be accurate in their work and to colour neatly.

f. Dictation

As a weekly exercise, dictation is useful in a number of ways. It gives the children regular practice in listening for sounds in the words they write, and it is a good way of monitoring the children's progress. Dictation also helps the children develop their independent writing, and encourages the slower writers to increase their speed.

Each dictation exercise consists of six words and three simple sentences. The words and sentences for each week are provided in the *Teacher's Book*. Both the words and the sentences help the children to revise the spelling pattern introduced that week. For example, if the focus for a particular week is the ‹igh› spelling of the /ie/ sound, then all the dictation words and sentences will feature this spelling pattern.

Lines are provided for dictation at the bottom of the children's *Pupil Book* pages. Begin by calling out the first word for the children to write down. When all the children have finished writing this word, ask one child to sound it out; as they do so, write the letters on the board. On reaching the sound of the week, the child should say the sound, for example /ie/, and then name the

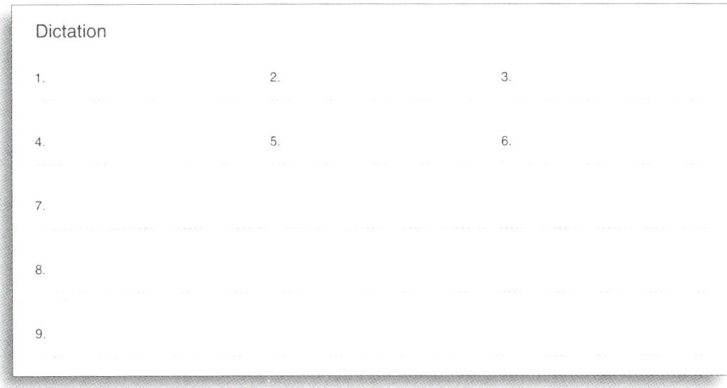

letters used to spell it, for example ‹igh›. The other children check whether they have written the word correctly and, if so, give themselves a tick. Read the remaining words and sentences one at a time and ask the children to write them on the lines in their *Pupil Books*. Remind the children that the sentences must begin with a capital letter and end with a full stop. It is also a good idea to point out any tricky words in the sentences. When all the words and sentences have been dictated, and if there is time, check the rest of the children's spelling, asking the children to sound out the regular words and spell the tricky words using the letter names.

Dictation tends to go slowly at first, and it may be necessary to reduce the number of words and sentences. However, the eventual aim is to get the children to write accurately, and relatively quickly, from dictation. When the majority of children have finished a word or sentence, move on to the next. The few children who have not finished should leave the item incomplete, and move on. This encourages them to get up to speed. For extra practice, these children could be given words for dictation homework.

Most of the dictation words are spelt regularly. The children should be able to spell these words correctly by listening for each sound and writing the appropriate letter(s). Dictation activities help the children to focus on hearing the sounds in words. They also help to prepare the children for using the more advanced spelling techniques, which involve analogy and word patterns. Most young children are unable to use analogy for reading or spelling until they have moved beyond the phoneme-blending stage and have a reading age of 7+ years.

Without regular practice, some children lose the ability to hear the sounds in words. This tends to be the case for those children who were slowest to acquire phonemic awareness in the first place. It is easy to identify spelling problems by looking at the children's independent writing. For example, if a child writes the word *play* as 'paly', this indicates that (s)he needs to be taught to listen more carefully to the sounds in words. Regular spelling practice is particularly important for such children.

A number of activities, which were introduced in the *Jolly Phonics Pupil Books*, can be used to improve phonemic awareness with a class, a small group, or an individual. They are as follows:

- The children listen carefully to a spoken word, and hold up one finger for each sound in that word. For example, the children hold up four fingers upon hearing the word *swing*, /s/, /w/, /i/, /ng/.

- The children orally 'chop' sounds off a word, one by one. For example, starting with the word *spot*, they say 'spot, pot, ot, t'.

- The children split words into their onset and rime, for example, 'str-eet', 'sp-oon', 'st-ar' and so on.

- The children split a word into its separate syllables, for example, 'luck-y', 'lem-on-ade', 'sun-flow-ers'.

- The children make new words by changing one sound at a time. For example, starting with the word *pin*, they say 'pin, pip, ship, sheep' and so on.

Grammar lessons

Unlike the spelling lessons, each grammar lesson has its own particular focus and the teacher's guidance varies accordingly. Despite this, the grammar lessons all follow the same standard format, which helps to give them a recognisable shape.

The format of the grammar lessons is as follows:

a. Aim

b. Introduction

c. Main Point

d. Activity Page

e. Extension Activity

f. Rounding Off

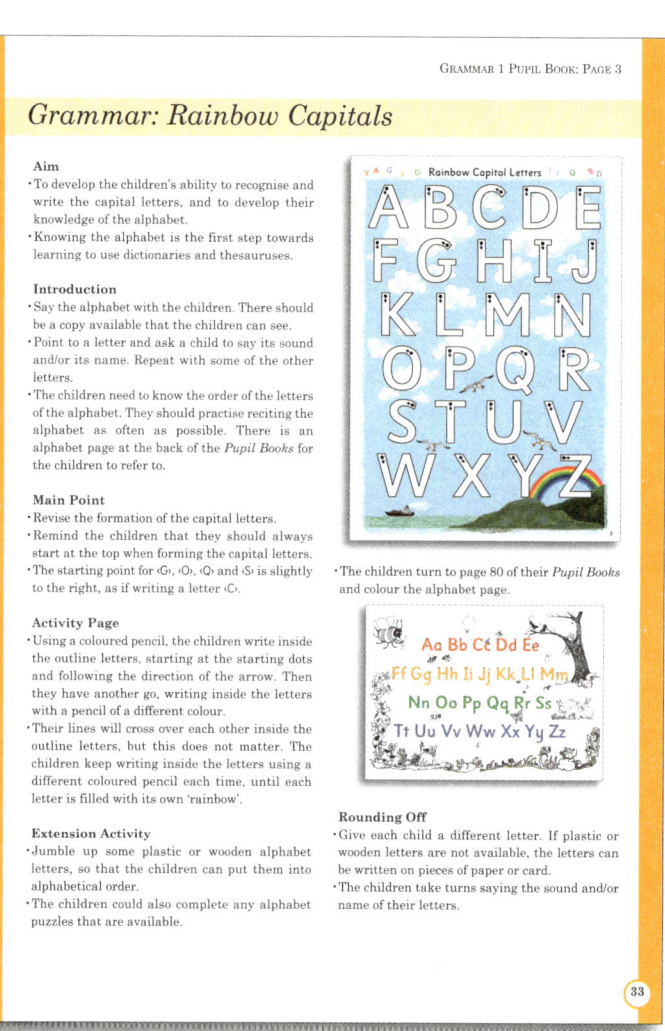

PART 2

Teaching with the Jolly Grammar 1 Pupil Book

The following pages provide detailed lesson plans and teaching guidance for use alongside the activity pages in the *Jolly Grammar 1 Pupil Book*. It is a good idea to read through the relevant teaching guidance prior to each lesson, and to prepare any additional materials that might be required.

For a typical spelling lesson, the teacher will need to prepare flash cards for the revision session and coloured pencils or crayons for the children's use. The teacher may also find it helpful to prepare a list of words featuring the spelling pattern of the week prior to the lesson. (The word banks on pages 25 and 26 can be used as a starting point for this list.) For lessons featuring the vowel sounds, the teacher may also like to have a puppet to hand, so that the vowels can be mimed, as illustrated on page 18.

The requirements for the grammar lessons are more varied. A number of the lessons require the children to have access to dictionaries, and often the class will need to be able to see an alphabet poster. (The alphabet poster at the back of each *Pupil Book* can be used if necessary.) Plastic or wooden alphabet letters can also be useful for alphabet work, and the *Jolly Grammar Big Book 1* is invaluable when introducing parts of speech. As with the spelling lessons, the children will need coloured pencils or crayons for each lesson. In addition, many of the Extension Activities require art and craft materials, in particular coloured paper and card, scissors, glue, paper plates and pictures from magazines.

Spelling: the ‹sh› spelling of the /sh/ sound

Spelling Test
- As the children have not been given any spelling words to learn yet, there is no spelling test in this lesson.

Revision
- Use flash cards to revise the digraphs introduced in *Jolly Phonics Pupil Book 1*: ‹ai›, ‹oa›, ‹ie›, ‹ee›, ‹or›, ‹ng›, ‹oo›, ‹oo›, ‹ch›, ‹sh›, ‹th›, ‹th›, ‹qu›, ‹ou›, ‹oi›, ‹ue›, ‹er› and ‹ar›.
- Use the flash cards, or the *Tricky Word Wall Flowers*, to revise the first set of tricky words. As each flash card is held up, the children should say the letter sound or read the tricky word.

Letter Sound
- Revise the ‹sh› spelling of the /sh/ sound.
- With the children, make a list of words that use this spelling and write the words on the board. (See word bank on page 25.) Ask the children to make up sentences using some of the words in the list.
- The ‹sh› words could also be written onto a big fish shape, which can then be used as a word bank for display.

Spelling List
- Read the spelling words with the children. As a class, say the sounds in the regular words, and say the letter names in the tricky words *I* and *the*.
- For *I*, remind the children that lower-case ‹i› (shy i) does not like to be alone, so capital ‹I› replaces it.
- When teaching *the*, remind the children that the ‹th› is regular, but they need to remember to add an ‹e› at the end to make the tricky word *the*.
- The last word in the list, *shampoo*, is longer than the rest. The children will find this word easier to spell if they split the word up into its two syllables, 'sham' and 'poo'.

am
get
clap
shop
fish
shut
wish
I
the
shampoo

Activity Page
- Practise the formation of the joined ‹sh›. The children write inside the outline ‹sh› on their page using the correct formation.

- This can be done several times, using a different colour each time.
- The children write an ‹sh› word in each fish and draw a picture to illustrate that word. Encourage the children to write and colour neatly. Colouring helps the children to develop their pencil control.

Dictation
- Read the words one at a time. The children listen for the sounds in each word, and write the words on the lines.

1. ship   2. shed
3. shelf   4. brush
5. rush   6. smash
7. I am on a ship.
8. She shops for food.
9. His toothbrush is red.

- Read the sentences one at a time for the children to write down.
- Remind the children that sentences start with a capital letter and end with a full stop. Point out the tricky words in the sentences.

Grammar: Rainbow Capitals

Aim
- To develop the children's ability to recognise and write the capital letters, and to develop their knowledge of the alphabet.
- Knowing the alphabet is the first step towards learning to use dictionaries and thesauruses.

Introduction
- Say the alphabet with the children. There should be a copy available that the children can see.
- Point to a letter and ask a child to say its sound and/or its name. Repeat with some of the other letters.
- The children need to know the order of the letters of the alphabet. They should practise reciting the alphabet as often as possible. There is an alphabet page at the back of the *Pupil Books* for the children to refer to.

Main Point
- Revise the formation of the capital letters.
- Remind the children that they should always start at the top when forming the capital letters.
- The starting point for ‹G›, ‹O›, ‹Q› and ‹S› is slightly to the right, as if writing a letter ‹C›.

Activity Page
- Using a coloured pencil, the children write inside the outline letters, starting at the starting dots and following the direction of the arrow. Then they have another go, writing inside the letters with a pencil of a different colour.
- Their lines will cross over each other inside the outline letters, but this does not matter. The children keep writing inside the letters using a different coloured pencil each time, until each letter is filled with its own 'rainbow'.

Extension Activity
- Jumble up some plastic or wooden alphabet letters, so that the children can put them into alphabetical order.
- The children could also complete any alphabet puzzles that are available.

- The children turn to page 80 of their *Pupil Books* and colour the alphabet page.

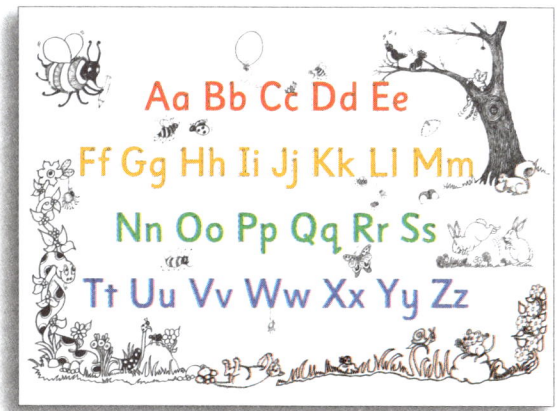

Rounding Off
- Give each child a different letter. If plastic or wooden letters are not available, the letters can be written on pieces of paper or card.
- The children take turns saying the sound and/or name of their letters.

Spelling: the ‹ch› spelling of the /ch/ sound

Spelling Test
- The children turn to page 74 of their *Pupil Books* and find the column labelled *Spelling Test 1*.
- In no particular order, call out the spelling words the children learnt last week:
  am, get, clap, shop, fish, shut, wish, I, the, shampoo.
- The children write these words on the lines for *Spelling Test 1*.

Revision
- Use flash cards to revise the following digraphs: ‹ai›, ‹oa›, ‹ie›, ‹ee›, ‹or›, ‹ng›, ‹oo›, ‹oo›, ‹ch›, ‹sh›, ‹th›, ‹th›, ‹qu›, ‹ou›, ‹oi›, ‹ue›, ‹er› and ‹ar›.
- Use the flash cards, or the *Tricky Word Wall Flowers*, to revise the first set of tricky words.

Letter Sound
- Revise the ‹ch› spelling of the /ch/ sound.
- With the children, make a list of words that use this spelling and write the words on the board. (See word bank on page 25.) Ask the children to make up sentences using some of the words in the list.
- The ‹ch› words could also be written onto a big treasure chest shape, which can then be used as a word bank for display.

Spelling List
- Read the spelling words with the children. As a class, say the sounds in the regular words, and say the letter names in the tricky words *he* and *she*.
- When teaching *he* and *she*, remind the children that the ‹h› and ‹sh› are regular, but the /ee/ sound at the end of these words is spelt ‹e›.
- The last word in the list, *chicken*, is longer than the rest. The children will find this word easier to spell if they split the word up into its two syllables, 'chick' and 'en'. It also helps the children remember the spelling if they emphasise the /e/ sound in the second syllable, pronouncing it to rhyme with *pen*.

if
hot
blot
chips
lunch
chest
much
he
she
chicken

Activity Page
- Practise the formation of the joined ‹ch›. The children write inside the outline ‹ch› on their page using the correct formation. This can be done several times using different colours.
- The children write a ‹ch› word in each treasure chest and draw a picture to illustrate that word. Encourage the children to write and colour neatly. Colouring helps the children to develop their pencil control.

Dictation
- Read the words one at a time. The children listen for the sounds in each word, and write the words on the lines.
- Read the sentences one at a time for the children to write down.
- Remind the children that sentences start with a capital letter and end with a full stop. Point out the tricky words in the sentences.

1. chin	2. much
3. chop	4. bench
5. such	6. lunch
7. I am rich.	
8. She sat on the bench.	
9. He had chips for lunch.	

Grammar: Sentence Jigsaws

Aim
- To develop the children's understanding of sentences.

Introduction
- Explain that sentences help to organise words and make their meaning clear.
- Read a passage aloud, ignoring all the punctuation.
- Ask the children what is wrong with what you have read. Ask them how they know where a sentence begins and where it ends.
- Read the passage again with the correct punctuation.
- Point out the capital letters at the beginning and the full stops at the end of the sentences.

Main Point
- Tell the children that sentences help organise spoken, as well as written, words.
- Select a few children and ask them to tell the class one sentence of news each. Choose one of the sentences and write it on the board without punctuation, for example:
    we went to the park
- Ask if this is a sentence and, if not, why not. Add in the capital letter and full stop.

Activity Page
- Read the first set of jumbled-up words on the children's *Pupil Book* page:
    pond. A swims duck the on
- Ask the children if the words make sense in this order. The children should say that they do not.
- Tell the children that they need to unscramble these words to make a meaningful sentence.
- The children should start by looking for the word with a capital letter. When they find it, the children write over the dotted word *A* at the beginning of their sentence, and cross out the jigsaw piece containing this word.
- The children use the remaining words to complete the sentence, using the picture as a clue.
- It helps if the children cross out each word as they fit it into their sentence.

- The children should be able to identify the last word of their sentence because it is followed by a full stop.
- The children unscramble the second sentence in the same way, and colour the picture.

Extension Activities
- Write some more jumbled-up sentences onto the board for the children to unscramble.

Rounding Off
- Go over the activity page with the whole class, so that all the children can see if they got the sentences right.

Spelling: the ‹th› spelling of the /th/ and /th/ sounds

Spelling Test
- The children turn to page 74 of their *Pupil Books* and find the column labelled *Spelling Test 2*.
- In no particular order, call out the spelling words the children learnt last week:
  if, hot, blot, chips, lunch, chest, much, he, she, chicken.
- The children write these words on the lines for *Spelling Test 2*.

Revision
- Use flash cards to revise the following digraphs: ‹ai›, ‹oa›, ‹ie›, ‹ee›, ‹or›, ‹ng›, ‹oo›, ‹oo›, ‹ch›, ‹sh›, ‹th›, ‹th›, ‹qu›, ‹ow›, ‹oi›, ‹ue›, ‹er› and ‹ar›.
- Use the flash cards, or the *Tricky Word Wall Flowers*, to revise the first set of tricky words.

Letter Sound
- Revise the ‹th› spelling of the voiced and unvoiced /th/ sounds. To help the children feel the difference between the voiced and unvoiced sounds, tell them to touch the front of their throats. With a voiced /th/ they will feel the vibrations of their vocal chords, whereas with an unvoiced /th/ they will not.
- With the children, make a list of words that use the ‹th› spelling and write the words on the board. Make sure that the list includes words containing the voiced /th/, for example, *this, that, then*, and words containing the unvoiced /th/, for example, *thin, thick, three*. Ask the children to make up sentences using some of the words in the list.
- The ‹th› words could also be written onto a big thought-bubble shape, which can then be used as a word bank for display.

Spelling list
- Read the spelling words with the children. As a class, say the sounds in the regular words, and say the letter names in the tricky words *me* and *we*.
- The last word in the list, *thinking*, is longer than the rest. The children will find this word easier to spell if they split the word up into its two syllables, 'think' and 'ing'.

| us |
| sad |
| flag |
| this |
| with |
| that |
| thank |
| **me** |
| **we** |
| thinking |

Activity Page
- Practise the formation of the joined ‹th›. The children write inside the outline ‹th› on their page using the correct formation. This can be done several times using different colours.
- The children write a ‹th› word in each thought bubble and draw a picture to illustrate that word. Encourage the children to write and colour neatly. Colouring helps the children to develop their pencil control.

Dictation
- Read the words one at a time. The children listen for the sounds in each word, and write the words on the lines.
- Read the sentences one at a time for the children to write down.
- Remind the children that sentences start with a capital letter and end with a full stop. Point out the tricky words in the sentences.

1. this	2. then
3. with	4. thin
5. think	6. thick
7. That moth is big.	
8. He is thin.	
9. She cut the cloth.	

Grammar: Correcting Sentences

Aim
- To develop the children's understanding of sentences.

Introduction
- The children practise reciting the alphabet. At this stage, the children may still need to see a copy of the alphabet for this activity, but once they know it well they will not need to look.
- Point to a letter and ask a child to say its sound and/or its name.
- Ask which letter comes after this one. Children find it much easier to name the following letter than the preceding one.

Main Point
- Explain that a sentence is not simply a line of words that begins with a capital letter and ends with a full stop. The words in between the capital letter and the full stop must also make sense. (This is a very simple working definition of a sentence, which young children can comprehend. As the children gain in understanding, this definition can be added to and refined.)
- Write some incorrect sentences on the board and read them with the children. Good examples include:

    the frog is green
    The cat ran up the.

- Ask why each line of writing is not a proper sentence.
- Correct the sentences with the class. (The first example needs only a capital letter and a full stop to make it correct. The second example has a word missing.)

Activity Page
- The children read each line of text, and decide whether it is a sentence or not. If the line of text is a complete sentence, the children copy it out underneath. If not, the children add in the missing words, capital letters, or punctuation marks, and write out the sentence correctly underneath.
- When the children have finished writing, they can colour the pictures.

Are these sentences correct? Write out each sentence correctly on the line.

1. the dog is spotty.

2. The duck swims on the.

3. I sleep in a bunk bed.

4. i like fish and. chips

5. He is playing football.

Extension Activity
- The children practise writing the alphabet, seeing how quickly they can write it.

Rounding Off
- Look at the activity page with the children. As a class, decide which of the sentences are correct.
- Discuss the incorrect sentences with the children, asking them why these lines of text are not complete sentences. Do the corrections with the children.

Spelling: the ‹ng› spelling of the /ng/ sound

Spelling Test
- The children turn to page 74 of their *Pupil Books* and find the column labelled *Spelling Test 3*.
- In no particular order, call out the spelling words the children learnt last week:
  us, sad, flag, this, with, that, thank, me, we, thinking.
- The children write these words on the lines for *Spelling Test 3*.

Revision
- Use flash cards to revise the following digraphs: ‹ai›, ‹oa›, ‹ie›, ‹ee›, ‹or›, ‹ng›, ‹oo›, ‹oo›, ‹ch›, ‹sh›, ‹th›, ‹th›, ‹qu›, ‹ow›, ‹oi›, ‹ue›, ‹er› and ‹ar›.
- Use the flash cards, or the *Tricky Word Wall Flowers*, to revise the first set of tricky words. As each flash card is held up, the children should say the letter sound or read the tricky word.

Letter Sound
- Revise the ‹ng› spelling of the /ng/ sound. Remind the children that this digraph can follow any of the vowels, not just ‹i›. Practise saying /ang/, /eng/, /ing/, /ong/ and /ung/.
- With the children, make a list of words that use the ‹ng› spelling and write the words on the board. Make sure that the list includes words containing ‹ang›, ‹eng›, ‹ong› and ‹ung›, as well as ‹ing›. (See word bank on page 25.) Ask the children to make up sentences using some of the words in the list.
- The ‹ng› words could also be written onto a big ring shape, which can then be used as a word bank for display.

Spelling list
- Read the spelling words with the children. As a class, say the sounds in the regular words, and say the letter names in the tricky words *be* and *was*.
- Encourage the children to use the 'say it as it sounds technique' when spelling *was*. Pronounce *was* as though it rhymes with *mass*.

in
leg
glad
ring
sang
strong
lung
be
was
length

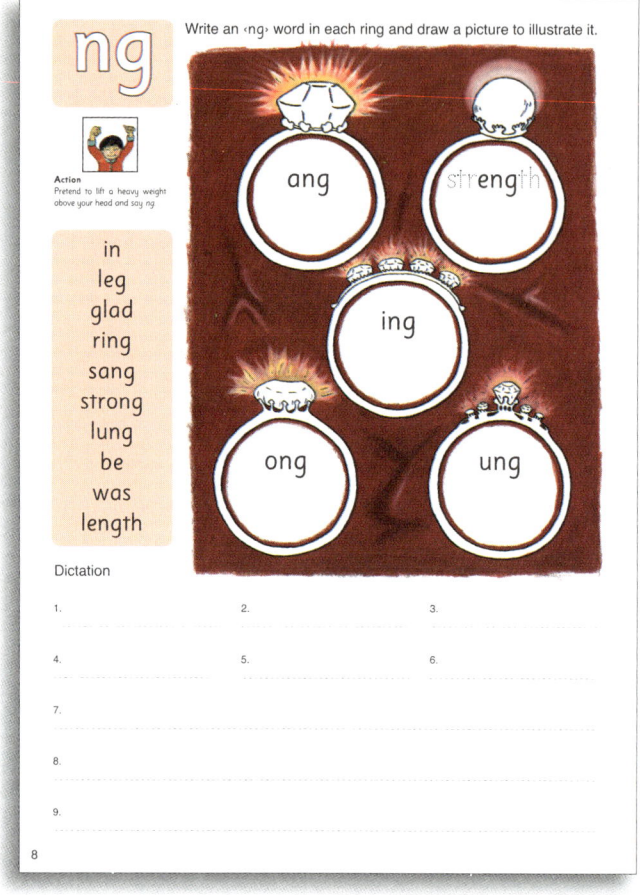

Activity Page
- Practise the formation of the joined ‹ng›. The children write inside the outline ‹ng› on their page using the correct formation. This can be done several times using different colours.
- The children write an ‹ng› word in each ring and draw a picture to illustrate that word. Encourage the children to write and colour neatly. Colouring helps the children to develop their pencil control.

Dictation
- Read the words one at a time. The children listen for the sounds in each word, and write the words on the lines.
- Read the sentences one at a time for the children to write down.
- Remind the children that sentences start with a capital letter and end with a full stop. Point out the tricky words in the sentences.

1. wing   2. song
3. bring   4. spring
5. sung   6. clang
7. The string was long.
8. She sang a song.
9. He had a sling on his arm.

Grammar: Capital Letters

Aim
- To develop the children's ability to recognise the capital and lower-case forms of each letter.

Introduction
- The children practise reciting the alphabet. At this stage, the children may still need to see a copy of the alphabet for this activity, but once they know it well they will not need to look.

Main Point
- Revise the formation of capital letters.
- Pay particular attention to those capital letters that are very different from their corresponding lower-case letters, for example, ‹A›, ‹B›, ‹D›, ‹E›, ‹F›, ‹G›, ‹H›, ‹N›, ‹Q›, ‹R›, ‹T› and ‹Y›.
- Write a letter on the board (capital or lower-case) and ask a child to say its sound and/or its name. Repeat with some of the other letters.
- Then write a lower-case letter on the board and ask a child to write the capital letter next to it. Repeat with other letters.

Activity Page
- At the top of the page, the children write the capital letters next to the lower-case letters. Make sure that the children start at the starting dots and use the correct letter formation.
- At the bottom of the page, the children pair up the balloons so that each capital letter is joined to its corresponding lower-case letter.

Extension Activity
- Provide each child with three or four plastic letters (wooden or cardboard letters could also be used). At this stage, the letters provided should be consecutive.
- See how quickly the children can put their set of letters into alphabetical order.

Rounding Off
- Give each child a different letter of the alphabet to hold.
- Recite the alphabet slowly.
- As each letter is called out, the child holding it stands up and moves to the front. The children at the front form an alphabet line, holding out their letters for the rest of the class to see.
- Once all the children come to know the alphabet better, this activity can be repeated with the children reciting the alphabet as a class.

GRAMMAR 1 PUPIL BOOK: PAGE 10

Spelling: the ‹qu› spelling of the /qu/ sound

Spelling Test
- The children turn to page 74 of their *Pupil Books* and find the column labelled *Spelling Test 4*.
- In no particular order, call out the spelling words the children learnt last week:
  in, leg, glad, ring, sang, strong, lung, be, was, length.
- The children write these words on the lines for *Spelling Test 4*.

Revision
- Use flash cards to revise the following digraphs: ‹ai›, ‹oa›, ‹ie›, ‹ee›, ‹or›, ‹ng›, ‹oo›, ‹oo›, ‹ch›, ‹sh›, ‹th›, ‹th›, ‹qu›, ‹ou›, ‹oi›, ‹ue›, ‹er› and ‹ar›.
- Use the flash cards, or the *Tricky Word Wall Flowers*, to revise the first set of tricky words. As each flash card is held up, the children should say the letter sound or read the tricky word.

Letter Sound
- Revise the ‹qu› spelling of the /qu/ sound. Remind the children that /qu/ is made up of two sounds: /k/ and /w/. If the children hear /kw/ in a word, they must remember to write ‹qu›.
- With the children, make a list of words that use the ‹qu› spelling and write the words on the board. Ask the children to make up sentences using some of the words in the list. The ‹qu› words could also be written onto a big duck shape, which can then be used as a word bank for display.

Spelling list
- Read the spelling words with the children. As a class, say the sounds in the regular words, and say the letter names in the tricky words *to* and *do*. Point out that the letter ‹o› makes an /oo/ sound at the end of both these words.
- The last word in the list, *squirrel*, is longer than the rest. The children will find this word easier to spell if they split the word up into its two syllables, 'squir' and 'rel'. It also helps the children remember the spelling if they emphasise the /e/ sound in the second syllable, pronouncing it to rhyme with *bell*.

on
but
plum
quick
quiz
queen
squid
to
do
squirrel

Activity Page
- Practise the formation of the joined ‹qu›. The children write inside the outline ‹qu› on their page using the correct formation. This can be done several times using different colours.
- The children write a ‹qu› word in each duck and draw a picture to illustrate that word. Encourage the children to write and colour neatly. Colouring helps the children to develop their pencil control.

Dictation
- Read the words one at a time. The children listen for the sounds in each word, and write the words on the lines.
- Read the sentences one at a time for the children to write down.
- Remind the children that sentences start with a capital letter and end with a full stop. Point out the tricky words in the sentences.

1. quit 2. quick
3. quench 4. quail
5. quest 6. liquid
7. She is quick.
8. The ducks quack.
9. The quiz was hard.

Grammar: Proper Nouns

Aim
- To introduce the children to the idea that there are different types of words, and that each type has a special name.
- In this lesson the children are introduced to proper nouns. Proper nouns are the names given to particular people and places, and to months and days of the week.

Introduction
- The children practise reciting the alphabet. Point to a letter and ask a child to say its sound and/or its name.
- Ask some of the children to write their names on the board. Check that they have all started their name with a capital letter.
- Ask the class what all the names on the board have in common. The answer is that all the names begin with a capital letter.
- Show the class some names in a storybook. Point out that these names also start with a capital letter. Explain that people's names always begin with a capital letter.

Main Point
- The special names given to particular people, places and things are called *proper nouns*.
- The children's names are proper nouns, and have a capital letter at the beginning to show how important they are. Other names are special too, and also need a capital letter. For example, the names of schools, roads, towns and countries are proper nouns, and are written with a capital letter at the beginning.
- To illustrate this, write out the school's address on a large envelope, or on the board. (The proper nouns should all have capital letters.)
- Read the address with the children and encourage them to identify the proper nouns, using the capital letters as a guide. There is also a page in the *Jolly Grammar Big Book 1* that introduces proper nouns.

Action: The action for proper nouns is to touch one's forehead with the index and middle fingers.
Colour: The colour for all types of noun is black.

Activity Page
- The children write inside the outlined words *Proper Nouns* using a black pencil.
- They draw self portraits in the first frame and write their names underneath, remembering to use a capital letter. There is space for their surnames as well. The children write the name of their teacher under the second frame, and draw a picture of him/her in the frame.
- The children write the school's address on the envelope.

Extension Activity
- The children write out the names of the other children at their table, or in their class.
- They look for the names of towns and countries in their atlases.

Rounding Off
- Call out a list of words, ensuring that the list includes some proper nouns. When they hear a proper noun, the children do the action; otherwise they keep still.

Spelling: the ‹ar› spelling of the /ar/ sound

Spelling Test
- The children turn to page 74 of their *Pupil Books* and find the column labelled *Spelling Test 5*.
- In no particular order, call out the spelling words the children learnt last week:
  on, but, plum, quick, quiz, queen, squid, to, do, squirrel.
- The children write these words on the lines for *Spelling Test 5*.

Revision
- Use flash cards to revise the following digraphs: ‹ai›, ‹oa›, ‹ie›, ‹ee›, ‹or›, ‹ng›, ‹oo›, ‹oo›, ‹ch›, ‹sh›, ‹th›, ‹th›, ‹qu›, ‹ou›, ‹oi›, ‹ue›, ‹er› and ‹ar›.
- Use the flash cards, or the *Tricky Word Wall Flowers*, to revise the first set of tricky words.

Letter Sound
- Revise the ‹ar› spelling of the /ar/ sound. With the children, make a list of words that use the ‹ar› spelling and write the words on the board. Ask the children to make up sentences using some of the words in the list. The ‹ar› words could also be written onto a big star shape, which can then be used as a word bank for display.
- In some regions, the letter ‹a› is pronounced with an /ar/ sound in words such as *class*, *path* and *father*. The children can learn the correct spellings of these words by using the 'say as it sounds' technique, pronouncing *father* to rhyme with *gather*.

Spelling list
- Read the spelling words with the children. As a class, say the sounds in the regular words, and say the letter names in the tricky words *are* and *all*. Point out that *are* is only tricky because children must remember to out the silent ‹e› at the end.
- The last word in the list, *farmyard*, is longer than the rest. The children will find this word easier to spell if they split the word up into its two syllables, 'farm' and 'yard'.

at
yes
slug
arm
hard
scarf
card
are
all
farmyard

Activity Page
- Practise the formation of the joined ‹ar›. The children write inside the outline ‹ar› on their page using the correct formation. This can be done several times using different colours.
- The children write an ‹ar› word in each star and draw a picture to illustrate that word. Encourage the children to write and colour neatly. Colouring helps the children to develop their pencil control.

Dictation
- Read the words. The children listen for the sounds in each word, and write the words on the lines.
- Remind the children that the /k/ sound at the end of *park* and *shark* is a kicking ‹k›. This is because both words have long vowel sounds.
- Read the sentences one at a time for the children to write down. Remind the children that sentences start with a capital letter and end with a full stop.

1. car   2. jar
3. part   4. start
5. shark 6. march
7. She has a red car.
8. I ran to the park.
9. A shark has sharp teeth.

Grammar: Common Nouns

Aim
- To introduce common nouns to the children.

Introduction
- Revise proper nouns with the class. Call out a list of words, ensuring that the list includes some proper nouns. When they hear a proper noun, the children do the action; otherwise they stay still.
- Remind the children that proper nouns need a capital letter at the beginning.

Main Point
- There is more than one type of noun. Tell the children that not all nouns are proper nouns.
- Remind the children that proper nouns are the names of specific people, places and things. Use the school as an example. Write the name of the school on the board. Explain that there is only one [read out school's name], but there are lots of schools. Remind the children that [read out school's name] is a proper noun. Then explain that the word *school* is also noun, but it is not a proper noun because there are lots of schools. Write the word *school* on the board (without a capital letter).
- Explain that these sorts of nouns are called *common nouns*, and do not need capital letters.
- Write some other common nouns on the board (without using capital letters), for example *chair, apple, dog, shop*. Explain to the children that these are also common nouns. Write the words *a, an* (the indefinite articles), and *the* (the definite article) in front of the common nouns on the board: *a chair, an apple, the dog, a shop*. Explain to the children that, if it makes sense to put *a, an,* or *the* in front of a word, then the word is probably a noun.
- It may help the children's understanding to tell them that nouns are things that can be photographed. However, this is true only of concrete nouns, and is not the case for abstract nouns, such as *happiness*.
- Call out some words. The children do the action for those that are common nouns.

Action: The action for a common noun is to touch one's forehead with all the fingers of one hand.
Colour: The colour for nouns is black.

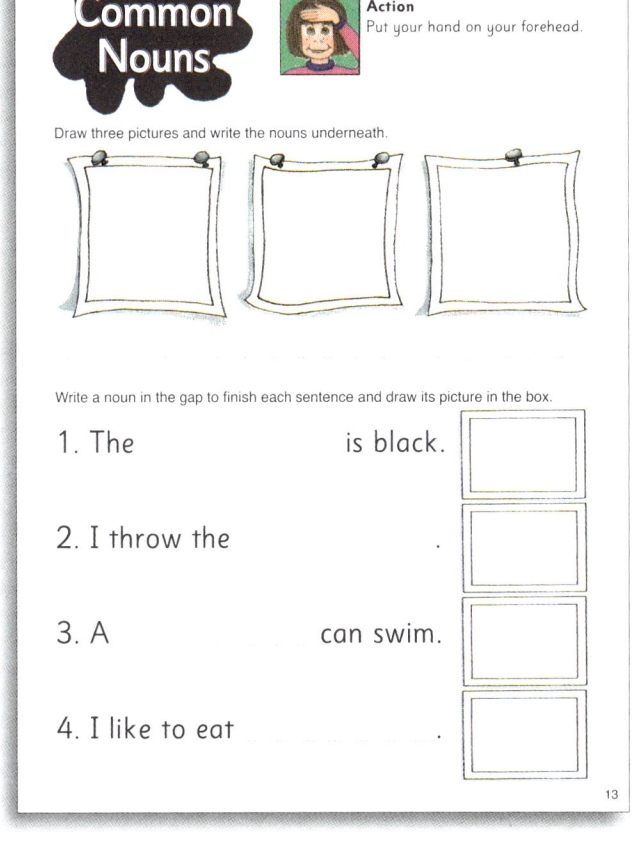

Activity Page
- The children write inside the outlined words *Common Nouns* using a black pencil.
- In each 'photograph', the children draw an object or an animal. If they struggle to think of objects to draw, encourage them to look around and choose three things that they can see. They write the common noun underneath each picture.
- The children complete the sentences by writing a common noun in each space. They read the sentence back to make sure it makes sense. They draw a picture of each common noun in the frames.

Extension activity
- The children draw pictures of things they see around them and write the common nouns underneath.

Rounding off
- Call out a list of words, including some proper nouns and some common nouns (avoid including abstract nouns). When the children hear a proper noun or a common noun, they do the appropriate action. Otherwise, they keep still.

GRAMMAR 1 PUPIL BOOK: PAGE 14

Spelling: Short Vowels

Spelling Test
- The children turn to page 74 of their *Pupil Books* and find the column labelled *Spelling Test 6*.
- In no particular order, call out the spelling words the children learnt last week:
  at, yes, slug, arm, hard, scarf, card, are, all, farmyard.
- The children write these words on the lines for *Spelling Test 6*.

Revision
- Use flash cards to revise the short and long vowels ‹a›, ‹ai›, ‹e›, ‹ee›, ‹i›, ‹ie›, ‹o›, ‹oa›, ‹u›, ‹ue›.
- Use the flash cards, or the *Tricky Word Wall Flowers*, to revise the second set of tricky words.

Letter Sound
- Revise the short vowels: /a/, /e/, /i/, /o/, /u/. The children could use their fingers to help them remember the sounds. They point to their thumb as they say /a/, their index finger as they say /e/, and so on. Many spelling rules relate to the short vowels, so the children need to be able to identify them in words.
- Say the words *bag*, *net*, *bin*, *box* and *mug*, and ask the children to identify the short vowel sound in each word. On the board, draw a bag, a net, a bin, a box and a mug. Call out some more CVC words with short vowel sounds, and ask the children to identify the short vowel in each word. As they do so, write the words in the container with the matching short vowel sound.

Spelling List
- Read the spelling words with the children. Say the letter names for the tricky words *you* and *your*.
- This week's spelling list is slightly different, as it features days of the week. The two longer words, *Wednesday* and *Saturday*, will be easier to remember if the children split them up into their three syllables, pronouncing the words, 'Sat-ur-day' and 'Wed-nes-day'. Remind the children that the /er/ sounds in *Thursday* and *Saturday* are both spelt ‹ur›.

dog
bran
Monday
Tuesday
Wednesday
Thursday
Friday
you
your
Saturday

Activity Page
- The children start with the first container on their page. They write over the dotted word *bag*, and write two more short /a/ words on the remaining lines. They fill each container with short vowel words in the same way.
- If the children struggle to think of words, you could provide a selection of CVC word cards for each table. The children read each word and copy it into the appropriate container. Ensure that there are at least three words for each vowel sound. (See word bank on page 25.)

Dictation
- Read the words one at a time for the children to write down.
- Read the sentences one at a time for the

1. robin   2. lemon
3. nutmeg 4. swam
5. rung   6. cobweb
7. The dog sits on the rug.
8. The fish swims in the pond.
9. She sings a song for her dad.

children to write down. Remind the children that sentences start with a capital letter and end with a full stop.

Grammar: Alphabetical Order

Aim
- To develop the children's knowledge of the alphabet.

Introduction
- The children need to be thoroughly familiar with each letter's position in the alphabet. This will improve their ability to find words in the dictionary.
- Show the children a dictionary and explain what it is for. Tell the children that if the words in a dictionary were divided into four approximately-equal parts, the letters would fall into the following groups:

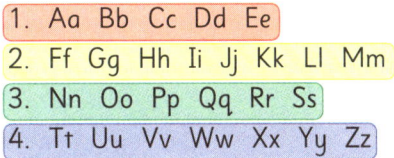

1. Aa Bb Cc Dd Ee
2. Ff Gg Hh Ii Jj Kk Ll Mm
3. Nn Oo Pp Qq Rr Ss
4. Tt Uu Vv Ww Xx Yy Zz

- The children practise saying the alphabet in these groups. They hold up one finger as they say the first group, pause, then hold up two fingers as they say the second group and so on.
- A copy of the alphabet divided into the four groups should be available for the children to see. They can turn to the alphabet page in their *Pupil Books* (page 80). Alternatively, there is also a copy in the *Jolly Grammar Big Book 1*.
- The four letter groups are incorporated in the *Jolly Dictionary*.

Main Point
- Point to, or hold up, letters (both capital and lower-case), and ask for their names and/or sounds.
- Ask the children which letter comes after the one being shown, and which letter comes before it.
- This activity is ideal for any spare moments, and needs to be repeated often if the children are to learn the alphabet thoroughly.

Activity Page
- The children trace over the dotted lower-case letters. Then they write the capital letters next to the lower-case letters.

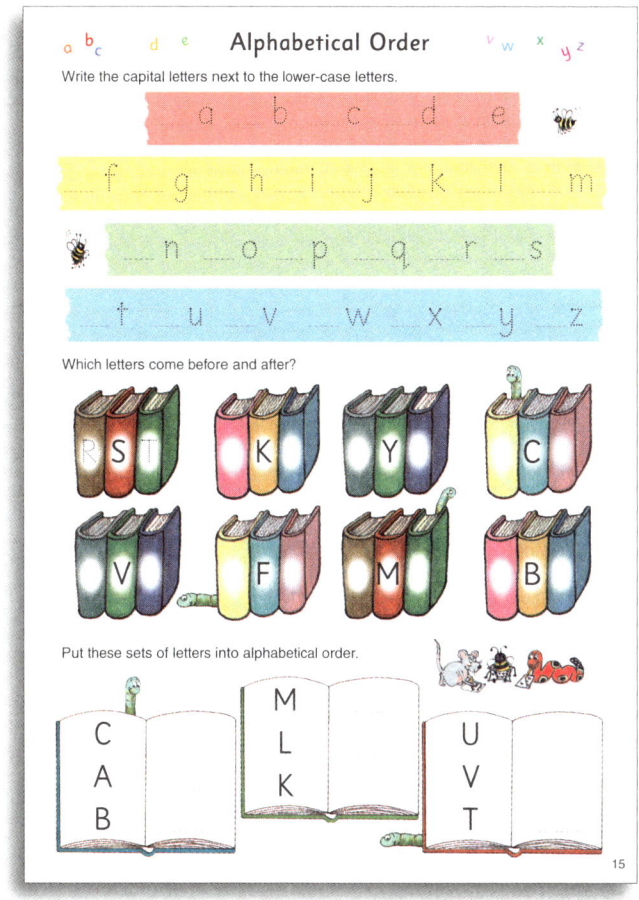

- For the second activity, the children write the letters that come before and after those in each set of books.
- Lastly, the children try putting each group of letters into alphabetical order. The letters in each group of three are consecutive, and should be written as capitals.

Extension Activity
- Write sets of letters on the board for the children to put into alphabetical order.

Rounding Off
- Give each child a different letter. If plastic or wooden letters are not available, the letters can be written on paper or card.
- Call out a letter. The child holding that letter stands up. Ask the class 'who has the letter that comes after this one, and who has the letter that comes before?' The children stand next to each other holding their letters in front of them.

GRAMMAR 1 PUPIL BOOK: PAGE 16

Spelling: the ‹ff› spelling of the /f/ sound

Spelling Test
- The children turn to page 75 of their *Pupil Books* and find the column labelled *Spelling Test 7*.
- In no particular order, call out the spelling words the children learnt last week:
  dog, bran, Monday, Tuesday, Wednesday, Thursday, Friday, you, your, Saturday.
- The children write these words on the lines for *Spelling Test 7*.

Revision
- Use flash cards to revise the digraphs introduced in *Jolly Phonics Pupil Book 1* and the short vowels ‹a›, ‹e›, ‹i›, ‹o› and ‹u›.
- Use the flash cards, or the *Tricky Word Wall Flowers*, to revise the second set of tricky words.

Letter Sound
- Introduce the ‹ff› spelling of the /f/ sound. When a /f/ sound comes at the end of a short word with a short vowel, it is usually written ‹ff›. However, the ‹f› is not doubled in the words *if* and *of*.
- Tell the children that they can remember the difference between the words *of* and *off* by listening to the sound at the end of the word. If there is a /f/ sound, as in *off*, then they must use ‹ff›, but if they hear a /v/ sound, as in *of*, they need only one ‹f›.
- With the children, make a list of words that use the ‹ff› spelling and write them on the board. Ask the children to make up sentences using some of the words. The ‹ff› words could also be written onto a big cliff shape, which can then be used as a word bank for display.

Activity Page
- Practise the ‹ff› formation. The children write inside the outline ‹ff› on their page using the correct formation. This can be done several times using different colours.
- The children write an ‹ff› word in each cliff and draw a picture to illustrate that word. Examples of ‹ff› words are provided in the word bank on page 25. Encourage the children to write and colour neatly. Colouring helps the children to develop their pencil control.

Spelling List
- Read the spelling words with the children. As a class, say the sounds in the regular words and say the letter names in the tricky words *come* and *some*.
- The last word in the list, *stuffing*, is longer than the rest. The children will find this word easier to spell if they split the word up into its two syllables, 'stuff' and 'ing'.

up
man
crab
off
cliff
stiff
cuff
come
some
stuffing

Dictation
- Read the words one at a time. The children listen for the sounds in each word, and write the words on the lines.
- Read the sentences one at a time for the children to write down.
- Remind the children that sentences start with a capital letter and end with a full stop. Point out the tricky words in the sentences.

1. off	4. gruff
2. cuff	5. ruff
3. huff	6. cliff
7. He can jump off the step.	
8. She ran up the cliff.	
9. We must not sniff.	

Grammar: *a* or *an*?

Aim
- To help the children learn when to use *an* instead of *a*.
- *A* and *an* are the *indefinite articles*.

Introduction
- Revise the five vowel letters ‹a›, ‹e›, ‹i›, ‹o› and ‹u›.
- Remind the children that all the other letters are called *consonants*.
- Revise the short vowel sounds /a/, /e/, /i/, /o/ and /u/, using a box and puppet to help the children listen for the sounds.
- For /**a**/, put the puppet **a**t the side of the box.
- For /**e**/, make the puppet wobble on the **e**dge of the box.
- For /**i**/, put the puppet **i**n the box.
- For /**o**/, put the puppet **o**n the box.
- For /**u**/, put the puppet **u**nder the box.
- The children can mime the short vowels. They make a fist with one hand, and pretend that this hand is the box and their other hand is the puppet. (See page 18 for further guidance.)
- Call out the short vowel sounds, or words with a short vowel in, and encourage the children do the appropriate action.

Main Point
- Write the following sentences on the board and read them one at a time with the class. Ask the children to identify, and underline, the nouns.
- Ask what is wrong with the sentences and allow the children to correct them.

   > An shark has an fin.
   > They saw a elephant at the zoo.

- Explain that in general, if a noun starts with a vowel sound, we use *an*, but if it starts with a consonant, we use *a*.
- If it makes sense to put *a*, *an*, or the definite article *the* in front of a word, then the word is probably a noun.
- Call out some nouns, and ask the children whether they would use *a* or *an* with each word. Ensure that some nouns in the list begin with a vowel, and some begin with a consonant.

Activity Page
- Look at the page with the children, asking them what each picture shows. If necessary, sound out and write the words on the board.
- The children can either just write *a* or *an* underneath each picture, or they can write the noun for the picture as well.

Extension Activity
- The children write down as many nouns as they can think of that begin with a vowel. They could use a dictionary to help them.

Rounding Off
- Look at the activity page with the children, and discuss their answers.
- Ask what other nouns beginning with a vowel the children have found.

Spelling: the ‹ll› spelling of the /l/ sound

Spelling Test
- The children turn to page 75 of their *Pupil Books* and find the column labelled *Spelling Test 8*.
- In no particular order, call out the spelling words the children learnt last week:
  up, man, crab, off, cliff, stiff, cuff, come, some, stuffing.
- The children write these words on the lines for *Spelling Test 8*.

Revision
- Use flash cards to revise the digraphs introduced in *Jolly Phonics Pupil Book 1* and the short vowels ‹a›, ‹e›, ‹i›, ‹o› and ‹u›.
- Use the flash cards, or the *Tricky Word Wall Flowers*, to revise the second set of tricky words.

Letter Sound
- Introduce the ‹ll› spelling of the /l/ sound. When an /l/ sound comes at the end of a short word with a short vowel, it is usually written ‹ll›.
- With the children, make a list of words that use the ‹ll› spelling and write them on the board. (See word bank on page 25.) Ask the children to make up sentences using some of the words.
- The ‹ll› words could also be written onto a big bell shape, which can then be used as a word bank for display.

Spelling List
- Read the spelling words with the children. As a class, say the sounds in the regular words and say the letter names in the tricky words *said* and *here.*
- The last word in the list, *windmill*, is longer than the rest. The children will find this word easier to spell if they split the word up into its two syllables, 'wind' and 'mill'.

red
win
drum
will
bell
doll
skull
said
here
windmill

Activity Page
- Practise the ‹ll› formation. The children write inside the outline ‹ll› on their page using the correct formation. This can be done several times using different colours.

- The children write an ‹ll› word in each bell and draw a picture to illustrate that word. Encourage the children to write and colour neatly. Colouring helps the children to develop their pencil control.

Dictation
- Read the words one at a time. The children listen for the sounds in each word, and write the words on the lines.

  1. ill 2. tell
  3. gull 4. doll
  5. smell 6. drill
  7. You must tell us all.
  8. She fell ill.
  9. He can spell well.

- Read the sentences one at a time for the children to write down.
- Remind the children that sentences start with a capital letter and end with a full stop. Point out the tricky words in the sentences.

Grammar: Plurals

Aim
- To develop the children's understanding of singular and plural, and to explain that the simplest way to make the plural of a word is to add an ‹s›.

Introduction
- Hide any copies of the alphabet.
- Sit the children in a circle, and ask one child to say the first letter of the alphabet. Go round the circle, with each child saying the next letter.
- Repeat this activity, choosing a different child to start each time, so that the children do not always say the same letter.

Main Point
- Hold up a picture of a dog and ask the children what it shows. Then hold up a picture of several dogs, and ask what this picture shows.
- Write *dog* and *dogs* on the board. Ask the children how the two words differ. Explain that nouns usually change when they describe more than one object. The name for nouns that describe one of something is *singular*, and the name for nouns that describe more than one is *plural*.
- The simplest way of making a plural is by adding an ‹s› to the end of the noun.
- Call out examples of singular nouns and ask the children to reply with the plural. For example, the teacher says 'one cat', and the children reply 'lots of cats'. Only call out nouns that are made plural by adding an ‹s›.
- Good examples include:
cat, rat, flag, hen, ant, tree, bird, bun, bed, drum, pen, map, leg, doll, van, cloud, duck, bat, car, boat, pet, book, sock, truck, train, ball, hat, bead, brick.

Activity Page
- The children read each noun and decide whether it is singular or plural. They illustrate each word, remembering to draw more than one item for the plural nouns.
- For the next activity, the children look at the pictures and decide what each picture shows. They write the noun underneath each picture, remembering to add an ‹s› to the noun if the picture shows more than one item.

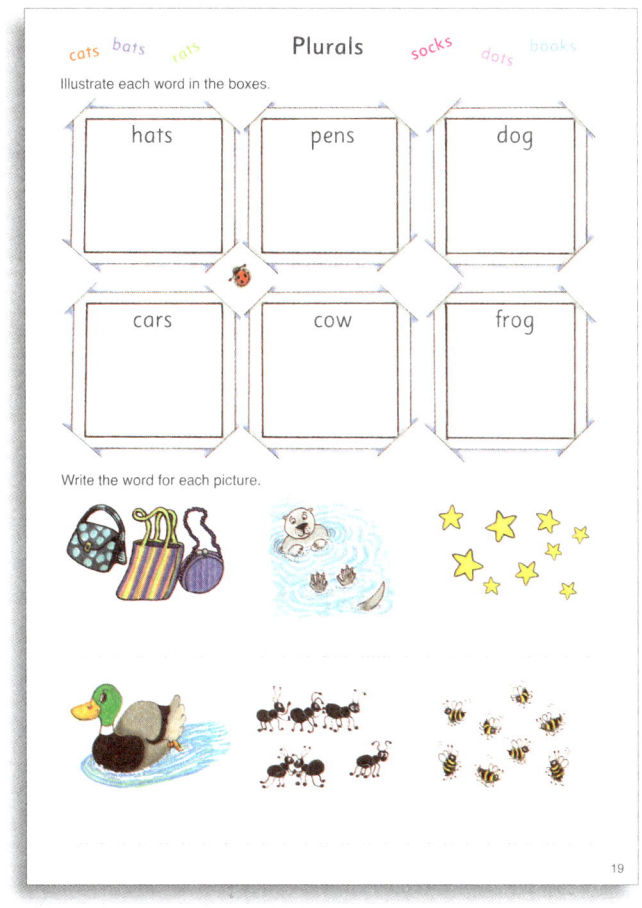

- The answers for the second activity are as follows:
  bag**s**   otter   star**s**
  duck   ant**s**   bee**s**

Extension Activity
- Write out some nouns with regular plurals on the board.
- Provide some paper or card for the children. The children choose a noun. On one side of their card, the children write the singular noun, and on the other side they write the plural. They draw a picture underneath each word, remembering to draw more than one item under the plural noun.

Rounding Off
- Look at the activity page with the class, checking which nouns are plural and which are singular.

Spelling: double ‹s› and double ‹z›

Spelling Test
- The children turn to page 75 of their *Pupil Books* and find the column labelled *Spelling Test 9*.
- In no particular order, call out the spelling words the children learnt last week:
  red, win, drum, will, bell, doll, skull, said, here, windmill.
- The children write these words on the lines for *Spelling Test 9*.

Revision
- Use flash cards to revise the spelling patterns taught so far, and the short vowels ‹a›, ‹e›, ‹i›, ‹o› and ‹u›.
- Use the flash cards, or the *Tricky Word Wall Flowers*, to revise the second set of tricky words.

Letter Sounds
- Introduce the ‹ss› spelling of the /s/ sound, and the ‹zz› spelling of the /z/ sound. When a /s/ sound comes at the end of a short word with a short vowel, it is usually written ‹ss›. Similarly, when a /z/ sound comes at the end of a short word with a short vowel, it is usually written ‹zz›.
- There are very few words with the ‹zz› spelling, which is why it is included here with ‹ss›.
- With the children, make a list of words that use the ‹ss› and ‹zz› spellings and write them on the board. (See word bank on page 25.) Ask the children to make up sentences using some of the words. The ‹ss› and ‹zz› words could also be written onto dress and bee shapes, which can then be used as a word bank for display.

Activity Page
- Practise the ‹ss› and ‹zz› formation. The children write inside the outline ‹ss› and ‹zz› on their page using the correct formation. This can be done several times using different colours.
- The children write an ‹ss› word in each dress, and a ‹zz› word in the bee. They draw pictures to illustrate each word. Encourage the children to write and colour neatly. Colouring helps the children to develop their pencil control.

Spelling List
- Read the spelling words with the children. As a class, say the sounds in the regular words and say the letter names in the tricky words *there* and *they*.
- The last word in the list, *crossroads*, is longer than the rest. The children will find this word easier to spell if they split the word up into its two syllables, 'cross' and 'roads'.

ox
run
from
buzz
cross
less
miss
there
they
crossroads

Dictation
- Read the words one at a time. The children listen for the sounds in each word, and write the words on the lines.
- Read the sentences one at a time for the children to write down.
- Remind the children that sentences start with a capital letter and end with a full stop. Point out the tricky words in the sentences.

1. hiss	2. buzz
3. fuss	4. jazz
5. cross	6. press
7. You can floss your teeth.	
8. She must press the bell.	
9. I will miss you.	

Grammar: Pronouns

Aim
- To introduce the personal pronouns to the children.

Introduction
- Tell the children a story without using any pronouns.
- For example: *Peter was having a birthday party. Peter wanted to blow up some balloons. Peter blew too hard and burst one of the balloons. Peter's sister laughed. Peter's sister helped Peter to blow up some more balloons.*
- Ask the children why the story sounds wrong.
- Tell the children that to avoid continually repeating names, we often use other, short words to take their place. These short words are called *pronouns*. Pronouns take the place of nouns.

Main Point
- Check that the children remember what a noun is. Tell the children the main pronouns and introduce the action for each one.

Actions: **I**: point to self
you: point to someone else
he: point to a boy
she: point to a girl
it: point to the floor

we: point in a circle to include self and others
you: point to two other people
they: point to the next-door class

Colour: The colour for pronouns is pink.

- Tell the children that the words *we* and *they* are always plural. The word *you* appears twice in the list. Make sure the children understand that it is singular in the first instance and plural in the second. This knowledge will help the children to understand the plural *you* when they come to learn other languages.

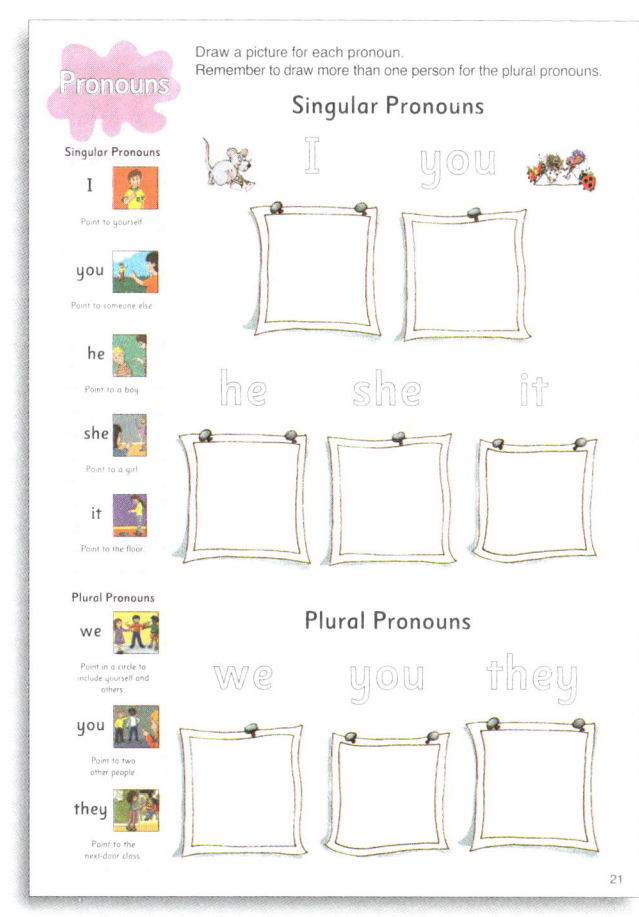

Activity Page
- The children write inside the outlined word, *Pronouns*, using a pink pencil. They write inside the outlined pronouns using the same colour, and then read the words.
- They illustrate the pronouns in the frames. In the frame underneath *I*, the children draw themselves. If the pronoun is a plural one, they must draw more than one person.

Extension Activity
- Ask the children to write a sentence using one of the pronouns.

Rounding Off
- Practise the pronoun actions with the class.
- Call out the pronouns and encourage the children to do the actions; then do the actions and ask the children to call out the pronouns.

Spelling: the ‹ck› spelling of the /c k/ sound

Spelling Test
- The children turn to page 75 of their *Pupil Books* and find the column labelled *Spelling Test 10*.
- In no particular order, call out the spelling words the children learnt last week:
  ox, run, from, buzz, cross, less, miss, there, they, crossroad.
- The children write these words on the lines for *Spelling Test 10*.

Revision
- Use flash cards to revise the spelling patterns taught so far, and the short vowels ‹a›, ‹e›, ‹i›, ‹o› and ‹u›.
- Use the flash cards, or the *Tricky Word Wall Flowers*, to revise the second set of tricky words.

Letter Sound
- Revise the ‹ck› spelling of the /c k/ sound. When a /c/ sound comes at the end of a short word with a short vowel, it is usually written with a ‹c› and a ‹k›.
- With the children, make a list of words that use the ‹ck› spelling and write them on the board. (See word bank on page 25.) Ask the children to make up sentences using some of the words.
- The ‹ck› words could also be written onto a big chick shape, which can then be used as a word bank for display.

Spelling List
- Read the spelling words with the children. As a class, say the sounds in the regular words and say the letter names in the tricky words *go* and *no*.
- The last word in the list, *broomstick*, is longer than the rest. The children will find this word easier to spell if they split the word up into its two syllables, 'broom' and 'stick'.

hop
fit
grin
duck
neck
clock
lick
go
no
broomstick

Activity Page
- Practise the formation of the joined ‹ck›. The children write inside the outline ‹ck› on their page using the correct formation. This can be done several times using different colours.
- The children write a ‹ck› word in each chick and draw a picture to illustrate that word. Encourage the children to write and colour neatly. Colouring helps the children to develop their pencil control.

Dictation
- Read the words one at a time. The children listen for the sounds in each word, and write the words on the lines.
- Read the sentences one at a time for the children to write down.
- Remind the children that sentences start with a capital letter and end with a full stop. Point out the tricky words in the sentences.

1. pack   2. luck
3. peck   4. brick
5. block 6. truck
7. Pack your bag.
8. The boys had a quick snack.
9. This will bring you luck.

Grammar: Initial Consonant Blends

Aim
- To develop the children's ability to read and write words with initial consonant blends.

Introduction
- Children often find it difficult to read words with initial consonant blends.
- Encourage the children to practise reading such words by blending the initial consonants first, and then the rest of the word. For example, the children should say '/dr/-/u/-/m/', rather than '/d/-/r/-/u/-/m/' when reading *drum*.
- The individual consonant sounds are not always easy to hear in blends, and the children need to practise listening to the blends for writing.
- Call out examples of words containing initial consonant blends, and ask the children to sound them out. Often the children will sound them out by saying the blend first and then the other sounds individually. Ask the children how they should write the blend sound. Ask them to hold up one finger for each sound.
- Good examples of words with consonant blends include:
flag, press, slip, stop, drum, clap, glen, crib, frog, slug, glad, green, swim, prod, club

Main Point
- Write the initial consonant blends (below) on the board, and practise reading them with the class.
- First, ask the children to say the sound the two letters make together, for example, /fr/, /gl/, /sm/.
- Then clear/cover up the board, and say each blend again for the children. Ask them to say the two sounds that make up each consonant blend. They should count each sound on their fingers.
- Initial consonant blends:
cl bl fl gl pl sl br cr dr fr gr pr tr sc sm sn sw tw sk sp st

Activity Page
- The children read the initial consonant blends around the edge of their page and write inside them.
- In the first box, they trace over the dotted ‹sl› to make the word *slug*.

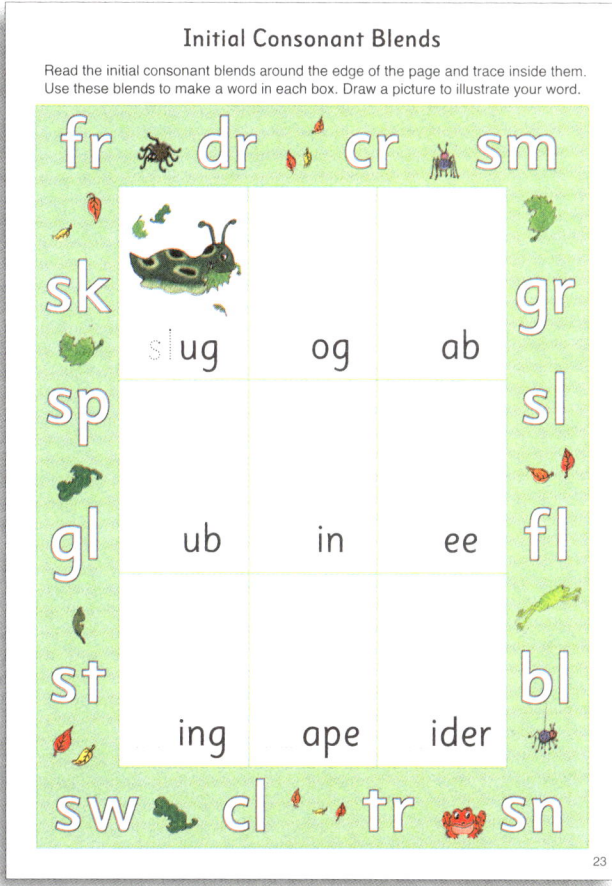

- They complete the remaining words by writing an appropriate consonant blend in each gap.
- If the children struggle with this activity, encourage them to pick one consonant blend, for example /tr/, and say it in each gap in turn until they find a word that makes sense, 'trog, trab, trub, trin, *tree*'.
- They write the ‹tr› blend next to the ‹ee› and illustrate their word in the box.

Extension Activity
- The children think of some other words that could be made with the consonant blends on their page.

Rounding Off:
- Look at the activity page with the class.
- Ask each child to read out one of the words he/she has made. Hopefully, the children will have come up with plenty of different words.

Spelling: ⟨y⟩ making an /ee/ sound

Spelling Test
- The children turn to page 75 of their *Pupil Books* and find the column labelled *Spelling Test 11*.
- In no particular order, call out the spelling words the children learnt last week:
  hop, fit, grin, duck, neck, clock, lick, go, no, broomstick.
- The children write these words on the lines.

Revision
- Use flash cards to revise the spelling patterns taught so far, and the second set of tricky words.

Letter Sound
- Remind the children that the main way of writing the /ee/ sound is ⟨ee⟩. However, when the /ee/ sound comes at the end of a word with more than one syllable, it is usually written with a ⟨y⟩.
- The letter ⟨y⟩ only makes a /y/ sound when it comes at the beginning, or occasionally in the middle, of a word. The rest of the time ⟨y⟩ makes a vowel sound. It can make the /i/ sound, as in *crypt*, the /ie/ sound, as in *cry*, and the /ee/ sound as in *cherry*. When ⟨y⟩ takes the place of a vowel, it can also change the sound of preceding vowels. For example, in the word *baby*, the ⟨y⟩ makes the ⟨a⟩ say /ai/. Two consonants are needed to make a 'wall' between the ⟨y⟩ and the other vowel. This is why the ⟨y⟩ spelling of /ee/ often comes after doubled consonants, as in *holly, berry, sunny*.
- With the children, make a list of words that use the ⟨y⟩ spelling of /ee/ and write them on the board. Ask the children to make up sentences using some of the words. The ⟨y⟩ words could also be written onto a holly leaf shape, which can then be used as a word bank for display.

Spelling List
- Read the spelling words with the children. As a class, say the sounds in the regular words and say the letter names in the tricky words *so* and *my*.
- The last word in the list, *family*, is longer than the rest. The children will find this word easier to spell if they split the word up into its three syllables, 'fam-i-ly'.

bed
wet
prod
holly
party
story
happy
so
my
family

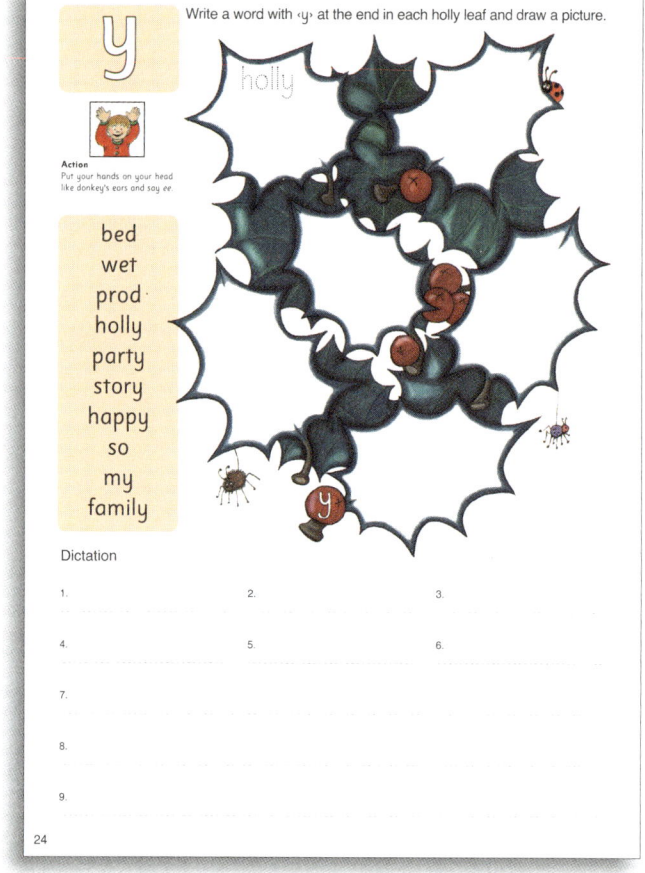

Activity Page
- The children write inside the outline ⟨y⟩ on their page using the correct formation. This can be done several times using different colours.
- The children write a ⟨y⟩ word in each holly leaf and draw a picture to illustrate that word. Encourage the children to write and colour neatly. Colouring helps the children to develop their pencil control.

Dictation
- Read the words one at a time. The children listen for the sounds in each word, and write the words on the lines.

  1. silly   2. fluffy
  3. fuzzy   4. mucky
  5. sleepy 6. frosty
  7. It was a very funny story.
  8. Sally has a party.
  9. The car was rusty and mucky.

- Read the sentences one at a time for the children to write down.
- Remind the children that sentences start with a capital letter and end with a full stop. Point out the tricky words in the sentences.

Grammar: Initial Consonant Blends

Aim
- To further develop the children's ability to read and write words with initial consonant blends.

Introduction
- Recite the alphabet with the children, pausing between each of the four groups. There should be a copy of the alphabet available for the children to see.
- Ask the children to find the vowels. Then ask them what all the other letters are called.
- Write some initial consonant blends on the board, and practise reading them with the class.
- Good examples incude:

cl bl fl gl pl sl br cr dr fr gr pr tr sc sm sn sw tw sk sp st.

Main Point
- Remove the consonant blends from the board.
- Call out each of the blends (listed above) for the children. Ask them to say the two sounds that make up each consonant blend. They should count each sound on their fingers.

Activity Page
- Look at the page with the children, asking them what each picture shows.
- The children write the correct word underneath each picture. There is a line for each of the sounds in the words, with a slightly longer line for digraphs.
- All the words begin with initial consonant blends.
- When the children have finished writing, they can colour the pictures. Encourage the children to write and colour neatly.
- The answers are as follows:

grin	*frog*	*drum*
crab	*skip*	*slug*
flag	*tree*	*star*
snail	*swing*	*spoon*

Extension Activity
- Write the folowing initial consonant blends on the board:

cl bl fl gl pl sl br cr dr fr gr pr tr sc sm sn sw tw sk sp st.

- Ask the children to think of some words that begin with each of the consonant blends. Encourage the children to look in storybooks and use dictionaries to find as many words as they can.

Rounding Off
- Look at the page with the class. Sound out and blend each word, for example, '/gr/ /i/ /n/, *grin*', '/sk/ /i/ /p/, *skip*'.

Spelling: Short and Long Vowels

Spelling Test
- The children turn to page 75 of their *Pupil Book*s and find the column labelled *Spelling Test 12*.
- In no particular order, call out the spelling words the children learnt last week:
  bed, wet, prod, holly, party, story, happy, so, my, family.
- The children write these words on the lines for *Spelling Test 12*.

Revision
- Use flash cards to revise the spelling patterns taught so far. Use the flash cards, or the *Tricky Word Wall Flowers*, to revise the third set of tricky words.

Letter Sound
- Revise the short vowel sounds /a/, /e/, /i/, /o/ and /u/. Vowel letters are different from consonants because they can use their names in words as well as their sounds; they can make the sounds /ai/, /ee/, /ie/, /oa/, /ue/, as well as the sounds /a/, /e/, /i/, /o/, /u/.
- In addition, the digraphs with at least one vowel letter, for example ‹or›, ‹oo›, ‹ou›, ‹oi›, ‹er› and ‹ar›, also make vowel sounds.
- Tell the children that all words in English must have at least one vowel sound. Call out some words. If a word contains a short vowel sound, the children do the appropriate short vowel action (see picture on page 18). If not, the children put their hands in their laps.

Spelling List
- Read the spelling words with the children. As a class, call out the sounds in the regular words and say the letter names in the tricky words *one* and *by*.
- The last word in the list, *colour*, is longer than the rest. The children will find this word easier to spell if they split the word up into its two syllables, 'col' and 'our'.

sad
let
trip
blue
orange
grey
black
one
by
colour

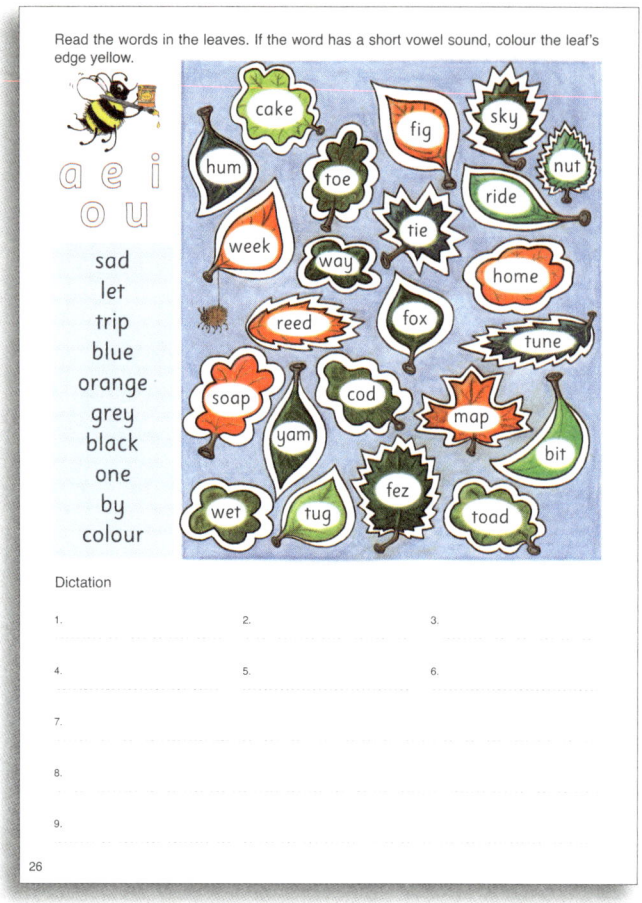

Activity Page
- The children trace inside the outline short vowels, using the correct formation.
- The children read the words in the leaves. If a word contains a short vowel sound, they colour the leaf's edge yellow.
- When the children have found all the short vowel words they could colour the remaining leaves' edges green. (The colours can be altered to suit.)

Dictation
- Read the words one at a time. The children listen for the sounds in each word, and write the words on the lines.
- Read the sentences one at a time for the children to write down.
- Remind the children that sentences start with a capital letter and end with a full stop. Point out the tricky words in the sentences.

1. pain   2. deep
3. lie   4. coat
5. rescue 6. coin
7. She sleeps in a bed.
8. We sat on the train.
9. The soap fell on the ground.

Grammar: Alphabetical Order

Aim
- To develop the children's knowledge of the alphabet, and their ability to use wordbooks and dictionaries.

Introduction
- The children practise reciting the alphabet, pausing between each of the four groups. They hold up one finger as they say the first group, then hold up two fingers as they say the second, and so on. A copy of the alphabet divided into the four groups should be available for them to see. Use the Alphabet Poster, or the alphabet in the *Jolly Grammar Big Book 1*.
- Call out some of the letters. Ask the children which group each letter belongs to, for example ‹s› is in the third group.
- Show the children a dictionary. Explain again that the words are listed in alphabetical order to make them easier to find. Knowing where a letter is in the alphabet will help the children work out where to look for it in the dictionary. Remind the children that the colours of the page edges in the *Jolly Dictionary* will also help them do this.

Main Point
- Give out dictionaries for the children to look at; they can share if necessary.
- Call out a letter and ask the children to find words beginning with this letter in the dictionary. Repeat the activity with other letters.
- This activity can be repeated in any spare moments. Children need a lot of practice at finding words in the dictionary. Once they improve, they can race each other to find letters.

Activity Page
- Using a different coloured pencil for each group, the children write inside the outline capital letters. They write the lower-case letters next to the capitals.
- The children need a dictionary for the next activity. They look up each letter, and find the first word listed that begins with that letter. They write this word on the line.
- Finally, the children put each group of letters into alphabetical order.

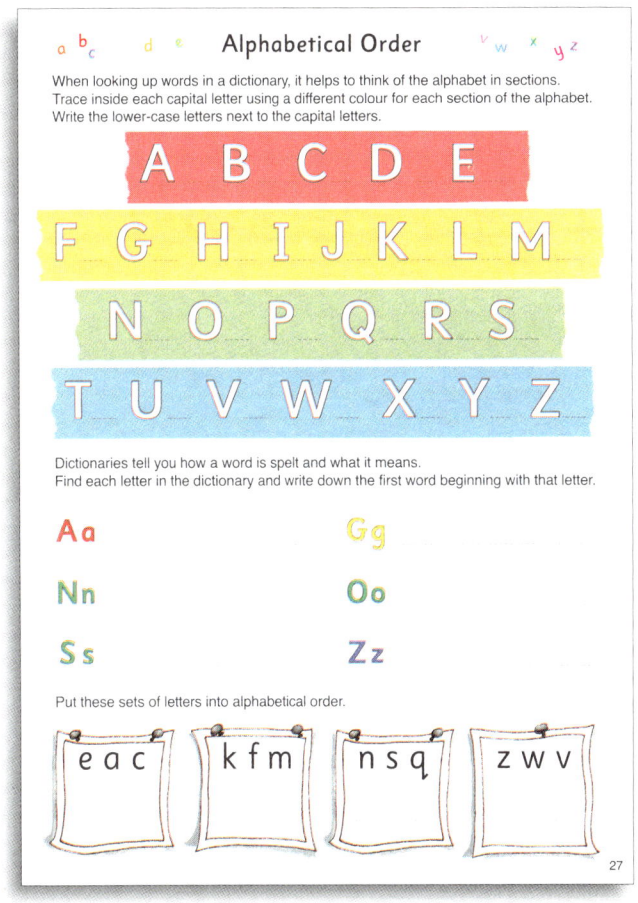

Extension Activity
- Let the children look through the dictionary, reading the meaning of words that interest them.
- Write some letters on the board for the children to find in the dictionary.

Rounding Off
- Look at the page with the children. Ask them which word beginning with ‹a› comes first in the dictionary. Then ask which word beginning with ‹g› comes first, and so on.
- As a class, put the sets of letters into alphabetical order.

GRAMMAR 1 PUPIL BOOK: PAGE 28

Spelling: the ‹a_e› spelling of the /ai/ sound

Spelling Test
- The children turn to page 76 of their *Pupil Books* and find the column labelled *Spelling Test 13*.
- In no particular order, call out the spelling words the children learnt last week:
  sad, let, trip, blue, orange, grey, black, one, by, colour.
- The children write these words on the lines for *Spelling Test 13*.

Revision
- Use flash cards to revise the spelling patterns taught so far, including the short vowels, ‹a›, ‹e›, ‹i›, ‹o›, ‹u› and the long vowels ‹ai›, ‹ee›, ‹ie›, ‹oa›, ‹ue›. Revise the third set of tricky words.

Letter Sound
- Remind the children that the main ways of writing the /ai/ sound are ‹ai›, ‹a_e› and ‹ay›.
- Revise the ‹a_e› spelling of the /ai/ sound, which can be referred to as '‹a› hop-over ‹e›'. It is important for the children to understand that the ‹e› in hop-over ‹e› digraphs is 'magic'. Although it makes no sound in the word, the ‹e› sends its magic over the preceding consonant, and changes the short vowel sound into a long vowel sound.
- With the children, make a list of words that use the ‹a_e› spelling and write them on the board. Ask the children to make up sentences using some of the words. The ‹a_e› words could also be written onto a bunch-of-grapes shape, which can then be used as a word bank for display.
- To illustrate the effect that a 'magic ‹e›' has in a word, try covering it up and then reading the word again. For example, *cape* becomes *cap* without the magic ‹e›.

Spelling List
- Read the spelling words with the children. As a class, say the sounds in the regular words and say the letter names in the tricky words *only* and *old*.
- The last word in the list, *baseball*, is longer than the rest. The children will find this word easier to spell if they split the word up into its two syllables, 'base' and 'ball'.

ran
hat
scar
came
grape
name
cake
only
old
baseball

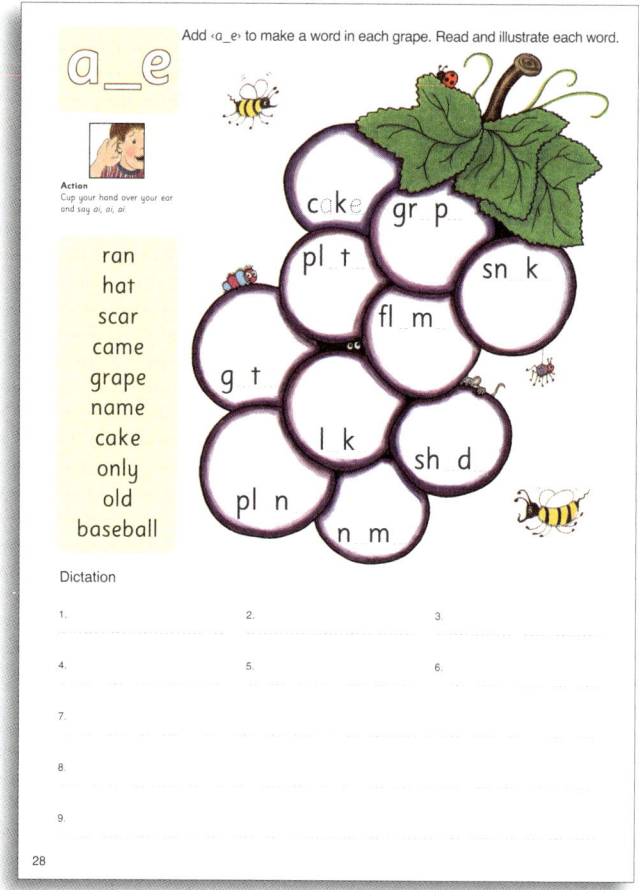

Activity Page
- The children write inside the outline ‹a_e› on their page using the correct formation.
- In each grape, the children write ‹a_e› in the gaps. They read the completed words and illustrate each one. Encourage the children to write and colour neatly. Colouring helps the children to develop their pencil control.

Dictation
- Read the words one at a time. The children listen for the sounds in each word, and write the words on the lines.
  1. mad 2. made
  3. at   4. ate
  5. scrap 6. scrape
  7. Dad made a cake.
  8. The gate is open.
  9. She was late.
- Read the sentences one at a time for the children to write down.
- Remind the children that sentences start with a capital letter and end with a full stop. Point out the tricky words in the sentences.

Grammar: Verbs

Aim
- To introduce verbs to the children.

Introduction
- Revise the parts of speech covered so far: proper nouns, common nouns, and pronouns.
- Call out some nouns (both proper and common) and ask the children to do the appropriate actions. As a class, say the pronouns with their actions.
- Write some sentences on the board. Good examples include:
    The bees play football.
    Bill kicks the ball.
    He scores a goal.
- With the children, identify the nouns and pronouns and underline the words in the appropriate colours, using black for nouns and pink for pronouns.

Main Point
- Explain to the children that there is another type of word called a *verb*. For young children, a verb can be defined as 'a doing word'.

Action: The action for a verb is to clench one's fists and move one's arms back and forth at one's sides, as if running.
Colour: The colour for verbs is red.

- Look at a picture that shows lots of things happening. There is a verbs page in the *Jolly Grammar Big Book 1*, which shows bees doing lots of different things. With the children, make a list of the verbs (the actions) illustrated in the picture.
- Generally, children will say the verbs in their gerund form; for example, they will say 'skipping, hopping, running' and so on. Teach the children that *skipping* is part of the verb *to skip*. Write the infinitive 'to skip' on the board. The root word in this instance is *skip*. Verb roots change according to the tense, to indicate when they take place.

Activity Page
- Help the children identify the verbs for the bees' actions in the first three pictures. The children complete the infinitives by writing the correct verb root on each line.

- They should not add ‹-ing› to the root.
- Read the next three verbs with the class, *to cry*, *to hop*, *to brush*. The children draw a bee doing each of these actions.
- Finally, the children think of three verbs by themselves, and complete the infinitives in the spaces. They illustrate the verbs in the flowers.

Extension Activity
- Provide a paper plate for each child.
- The children choose one verb each, They draw a bee 'doing' their verb in the middle of the plate.
- They then cut out petal shapes from coloured paper and stick them around the edge of the plate to make a flower. These can be used to make a wall display.

Rounding Off
- Look at the activity page with the children. Ask them which verbs they wrote.
- Call out a list of words, including proper nouns, common nouns and verbs. The children do the appropriate action for each word.

GRAMMAR 1 PUPIL BOOK: PAGE 30

Spelling: the ‹i_e› spelling of the /ie/ sound

Spelling Test
- The children turn to page 76 of their *Pupil Books* and find the column labelled *Spelling Test 14*.
- In no particular order, call out the spelling words the children learnt last week:
  ran, hat, scar, came, grape, name, cake, only, old, pavement.
- The children write these words on the lines.

Revision
- Use flash cards to revise the spelling patterns taught so far, including the short vowels and the long vowels. Revise the third set of tricky words.

Letter Sound
- Remind the children that the main ways of writing the /ie/ sound are ‹ie›, ‹i_e›, ‹igh› and ‹y›.
- Revise the ‹i_e› spelling of the /ie/ sound, which can be referred to as '‹i› hop-over ‹e›'. It is important for the children to understand that the ‹e› in hop-over ‹e› digraphs is 'magic'. Although it makes no sound in the word, the ‹e› sends its magic over the preceding consonant, and changes the short vowel sound into a long vowel sound.
- With the children, make a list of words that use the ‹i_e› spelling and write them on the board. Ask the children to make up sentences using some of the words. The ‹i_e› words could also be written onto a big kite shape, which can then be used as a word bank for display.
- To illustrate the effect that a 'magic ‹e›' has in a word, try covering it up and then reading the word again. For example, *ride* becomes *rid* without the magic ‹e›.

Spelling List
- Read the spelling words with the children. As a class, say the sounds in the regular words and say the letter names in the tricky words *like* and *have*. *Like* is not really a tricky word, but the children must remember that the /ie/ sound is written with the ‹i_e› spelling. Explain that *have* has a silent ‹e› at the end. The ‹e› is there because words in English do not end in ‹v›.

six
pad
smell
bike
time
smile
prize
like
have
bridesmaid

- The last word in the list, *bridesmaid*, is longer than the rest. The children will find this word easier to spell if they split the word up into its two syllables, 'brides' and 'maid'.

Activity Page
- The children write inside the outline ‹i_e› on their page using the correct formation.
- In each kite, the children write ‹i_e› in the gaps. They read the completed words and illustrate each one. Encourage the children to write and colour neatly. Colouring helps the children to develop their pencil control.

Dictation
- Read the words one at a time. The children listen for the sounds in each word, and write the words on the lines.
- Read the sentences one at a time for the children to write down.

1. wine   2. win
3. slid   4. slide
5. spine 6. spin
7. I like my prize.
8. She has a red bike.
9. They had a kite.

Grammar: Conjugating Verbs

Aim
- To develop the children's knowledge of verbs.

Introduction
- Revise verbs. Call out words, including proper nouns, common nouns and verbs, and ask the children to do the appropriate actions.

  N.B. Many common verbs can also be nouns. For example, the word *smile* can be a verb 'to smile', or a noun 'the smile'. For the purposes of this lesson, try to use only those verbs which cannot also be nouns.
- Good examples of verbs which cannot be used as nouns are as follows:
  to eat, to clean, to feel, to fill, to draw, to live, to make, to give, to hear, to sew, to wear, to bring
- Write some sentences on the board. With the children, identify the proper nouns, common nouns, pronouns and verbs, and underline them in the correct colours.
- Example sentences include:
  Mum drives a car.   We help Mum clean it.

Main Point
- Revise pronouns and their actions (see pages 7 to 8).
- Choose a verb, for example *to eat*, and tell the class that they are going to join it to the pronouns.
- With the children, say:

  I eat, you eat, he eats, she eats, it eats, we eat, you eat, they eat.
- This is called *conjugating a verb*. Tell the children that for *he*, *she* and *it*, (the third person singular pronouns), they must add an ‹s› to the verb root.
- Ask the children to think of some more verbs, and conjugate them with the appropriate actions for the pronouns and verbs.

Activity Page
- The children write inside the outlined word, *Verbs*, in red.
- Then, either choose a verb as a class, or let each child choose a different verb. The children write their verb on the line provided at the top of the page, and use a pink pencil to underline the pronouns. They write their verb beside each pronoun.

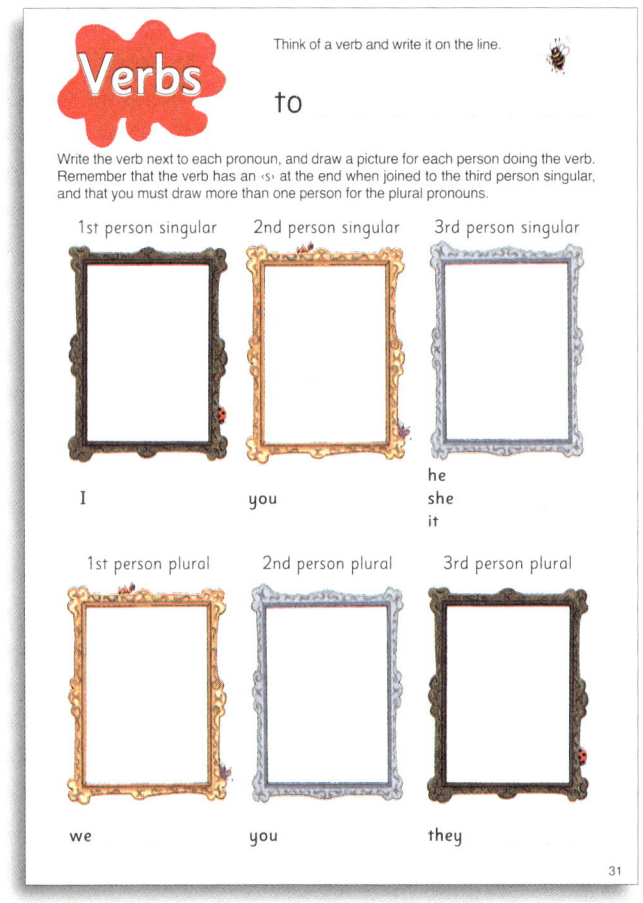

- Remind the children that for *he*, *she* and *it*, an ‹s› must be added to the verb root.
- Point out that *I*, *you*, *he*, *she* and *it* are singular, and that *we*, *you* and *they* are plural.
- The children draw a picture to illustrate the person, or people, doing their verb.

Extension Activity
- Ask the children to think of other verbs and conjugate them.

Rounding Off
- Do the action for a particular pronoun, and then mime a verb. Encourage the children to work out what you are 'saying'. For example, point to a girl and pretend to write something; the children answer *She writes*.

GRAMMAR 1 PUPIL BOOK: PAGE 32

Spelling: the ‹o_e› spelling of the /oa/ sound

Spelling Test
- The children turn to page 76 of their *Pupil Books* and find the column labelled *Spelling Test 15*.
- In no particular order, call out the spelling words the children learnt last week:
  six, pad, smell, bike, time, smile, prize, like, have, bridesmaid
- The children write these words on the lines.

Revision
- Use flash cards to revise the spelling patterns taught so far, including the short vowels and the long vowels. Revise the third set of tricky words.

Letter Sound
- Remind the children that the main ways of writing the /oa/ sound are ‹oa›, ‹o_e› and ‹ow›.
- Revise the ‹o_e› spelling of the /oa/ sound, which can be referred to as '‹o› hop-over ‹e›'. It is important for the children to understand that the ‹e› in hop-over ‹e› digraphs is 'magic'. Although it makes no sound in the word, the ‹e› sends its magic over the preceding consonant, and changes the short vowel sound into a long vowel sound.
- With the children, make a list of words that use the ‹o_e› spelling and write them on the board. Ask the children to make up sentences using some of the words. The ‹o_e› words could also be written onto a big tadpole shape, which can then be used as a word bank for display.
- To illustrate the effect that a 'magic ‹e›' has in a word, try covering it up and then reading the word again. For example, *hope* becomes *hop* without the magic ‹e›.

Spelling List
- Read the spelling words with the children. As a class, say the sounds in the regular words and say the letter names in the tricky words *live* and *give*. Tell the children to be careful when reading *live*, as it could have either an /ie/ sound or a short /i/ sound. They will have to work out which word is meant from the context. Explain that, despite the ‹i_e› spelling, *give* has a short /i/ sound in the middle.

| cod |
| lot |
| snap |
| bone |
| nose |
| home |
| globe |
| **live** |
| **give** |
| tadpole |

- The last word in the list, *tadpole*, is longer than the rest. The children will find this word easier to spell if they split the word up into its two syllables, 'tad' and 'pole'.

Activity Page
- The children write inside the outline ‹o_e› on their page using the correct formation.
- In each tadpole, the children write ‹o_e› in the gaps. They read the completed words and illustrate each one. Encourage the children to write and colour neatly. Colouring helps the children to develop their pencil control.

Dictation
- Read the words one at a time. The children listen for the sounds in each word, and write the words on the lines.
- Read the sentences one at a time for the children to write down.

1. rode 2. rod
3. hope 4. hop
5. note 6. not
7. It is time to go home.
8. Those roses are pink.
9. The mole is in his hole.

Grammar: Past Tense Verbs

Aim
- To develop the children's knowledge of the past tense. Explain that the simple past tense of a regular verb is formed by adding ‹ed› to the verb root.

Introduction
- Call out words, including proper and common nouns, pronouns and verbs, for the children to do the actions. When calling out a word that can function as either a verb or a noun, for example *smile*, see which action the children do. Explain that both actions are right, as the word *smile* can be either a verb or a noun.
- Ask the children how they would know whether a word was a noun or a verb if they read it in a sentence. Write two sentences on the board. In one sentence the word should function as a verb, and in the other it should function as a noun.
- For example, for the word *race*, write the following two sentences:
    She races up the hill. (verb)
    She runs in a race. (noun)
- With the children, look at the words in the sentences. Decide which parts of speech they are, and underline them in the appropriate colours. It is important that the children realise that a word can function as more than one part of speech, and that they need to look at the context to see how it is being used.

Main Point
- Explain that verbs often change to show when the action takes place. So far, the verbs taught have all been in the present tense, which means they describe actions taking place now. If the verb describes an action that has already taken place, it should be in the past tense. So, 'Today I wish' is in the present tense, but 'Yesterday I wished' is in the past tense.

Present Tense Action: Point towards the floor with the palm of the hand.
Past Tense Action: Point backwards over the shoulder with a thumb.
Colour: The colour for verbs is red.

- The past tense of a regular verb is made by adding the suffix ‹ed› to the root. If the verb root ends with an ‹e›, the children should remove the ‹e› before adding ‹ed›.

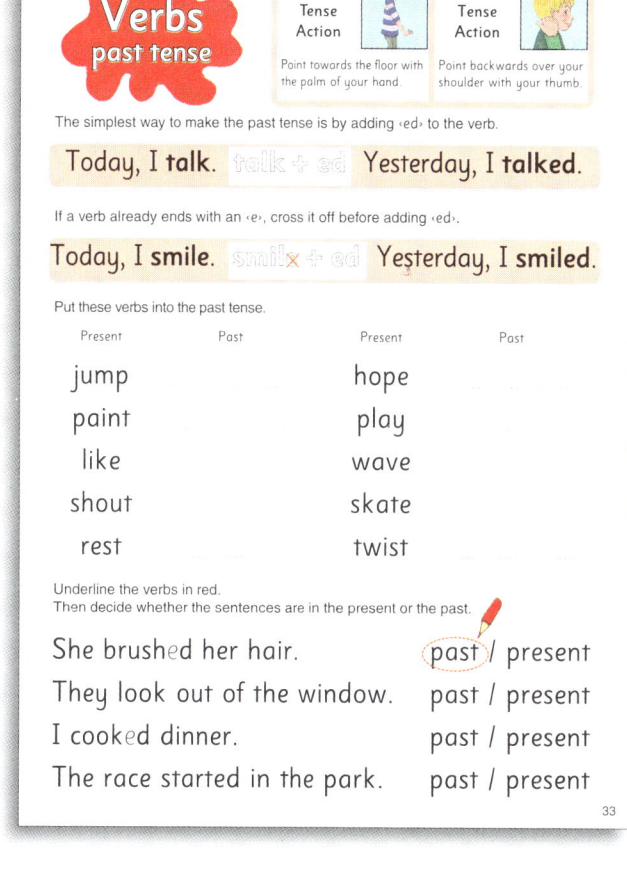

- The ‹ed› ending can make three different sounds, either /id/ as in *hated*, /d/ as in *saved*, or /t/ as in *missed*. Call out some verbs in the present and past tenses and encourage the children to do the actions to indicate the tense.

Activity Page
- With the children, read through the activity page. For the first activity, the children read the list of verbs in the present tense, and write them out in the past tense.
- For the second activity the children read the sentences and decide if they are in the present or past tense.

Extension Activity
- Write some sentences on the board in the present tense, and ask the children how they should change the sentences to make them in the past tense.

Rounding Off
- Read through the activity page with the children and check that they can form and identify regular verbs in the simple past tense.

Spelling: the ‹u_e› spelling of the /ue/ sound

Spelling Test
- The children turn to page 76 of their *Pupil Books* and find the column labelled *Spelling Test 16*.
- In no particular order, call out the spelling words the children learnt last week:
  cod, lot, snap, bone, nose, home, globe, live, give, tadpole.
- The children write these words on the lines.

Revision
- Use flash cards to revise the spelling patterns taught so far, including the short vowels and the long vowels. Revise the third set of tricky words.

Letter Sound
- Remind the children that the main ways of writing the /ue/ sound are ‹ue›, ‹u_e› and ‹ew›. The ‹u_e› is a difficult spelling because it can make the /oo/ sound, as in *rude*, or the /ue/ sound, as in *fuse*.
- Revise the ‹u_e› spelling of the /ue/ sound, which can be referred to as '‹u› hop-over ‹e›'. It is important for the children to understand that the ‹e› in hop-over ‹e› digraphs is 'magic'. Although it makes no sound in the word, the ‹e› sends its magic over the preceding consonant, and changes the short vowel sound into a long vowel sound.
- With the children, make a list of words that use the ‹u_e› spelling and write them on the board. Ask the children to make up sentences using some of the words. The ‹u_e› words could also be written onto a big musical note shape, which can then be used as a word bank for display.
- To illustrate the effect that a 'magic ‹e›' has in a word, try covering it up and then reading the word again. For example, *use* becomes *us* without the magic ‹e›.

Spelling List
- Read the spelling words with the children. As a class, say the sounds in the regular words and say the letter names in the tricky words *little* and *down*.
- The last word in the list, *useless*, is longer than the rest. The children will find this word easier to spell if they split the word up into its two syllables, 'use' and 'less'.

bus
pot
swim
cube
tune
used
excuse
little
down
useless

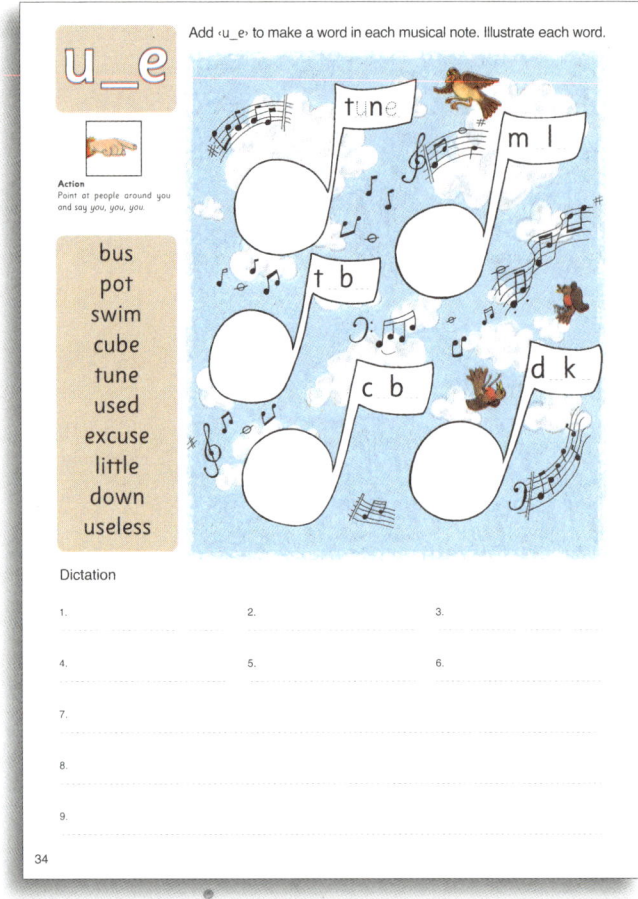

Activity Page
- The children write inside the outline ‹u_e› on their page using the correct formation.
- In each note of the 'tune', the children write ‹u_e› in the gaps. They read the completed words and illustrate each one. Encourage the children to write and colour neatly. Colouring helps the children to develop their pencil control.

Dictation
- Read the words one at a time. The children listen for the sounds in each word, and write the words on the lines.

  1. us   2. use
  3. cub   4. cube
  5. tube   6. tub
  7. They broke a rule.
  8. Soon we will see the duke.
  9. The girl played a tune.

- Read the sentences one at a time for the children to write down.
- Remind the children that sentences start with a capital letter and end with a full stop. Point out the tricky words in the sentences.

Grammar: The Doubling Rule

Aim
- To develop the children's ability to recognise the short vowels in words, so that they are able to work out when to apply the doubling rule before adding ‹-ed›.

Introduction
- Say the alphabet with the children, pausing between each of the four groups. See if the children can recite the alphabet without reading it.
- Revise the short vowels.
- Revise the present and past tenses. Call out some verbs in the present and past tenses and encourage the children to do the appropriate actions (see pages 9 and 10).

Main Point
- Explain that the endings that are added to words are called *suffixes*.
- If a word has a short vowel sound, it is important to be careful when adding a suffix that starts with a vowel, such as ‹-ed›. This is because the ‹e› in the suffix behaves like a magic ‹e›, and changes the vowel sound in the word. For example, if ‹-ed› is added to *hop* it becomes *hoped*. The short /o/ sound becomes a long /oa/ sound, and this completely changes the meaning of the word. To avoid mistakes like this, we use the 'doubling rule'. The consonant at the end of the root word is doubled to make a 'wall'. The magic from the ‹e› cannot jump over a wall of more than one letter.
- Draw the children's attention to the illustration of the doubling rule wall in the top right-hand corner of their page. The children are unlikely to remember this rule immediately, but will learn it gradually with enough revision.
- Examples of verb roots to which the doubling rule applies include:
  fit, slip, skip, clap, grab, hop, wag, bat, pat, peg, rip, nod, hug, hum.
- If the children ask about a word like *stamped*, explain that this word already has a 'wall' made by the two consonants ‹m› and ‹p›. Words that do not have short vowel sounds, for example *look*, *play* and *bark*, do not need a 'wall' and so the children do not need to double the last consonant.

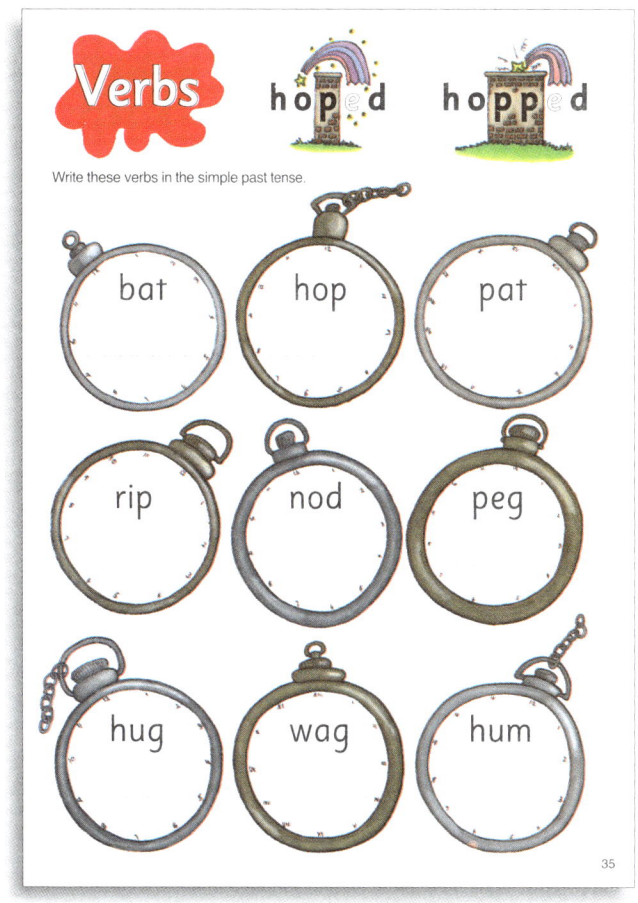

Activity Page
- The children read the verb roots in each fob watch and write the verbs in the past tense underneath, remembering to apply the doubling rule.

Extension Activity
- Call out some verbs. The children listen for the vowel sounds. For those verbs that have a short vowel sound, the children do the actions for Inky and the box (see illustration on page 18). For those verbs that do not have a short vowel sound, the children put their hands in their laps.

Rounding Off
- Read through the activity page with the children.
- Check that they understand when the doubling rule should be applied to a word.

Spelling: the ‹wh› spelling of the /w/ sound

Spelling Test
- The children turn to page 76 of their *Pupil Books* and find the column labelled *Spelling Test 17*.
- In no particular order, call out the spelling words the children learnt last week:
  bus, pot, swim, cube, tune, used, excuse, little, down, useless.
- The children write these words on the lines for *Spelling Test 17*.

Revision
- Use flash cards to revise the spelling patterns taught so far, including the short and long vowels.
- Use the flash cards, or the *Tricky Word Wall Flowers*, to revise the third set of tricky words

Letter Sound
- Introduce the ‹wh› spelling of the /w/ sound.
- With the children, make a list of words that use the ‹wh› spelling and write them on the board. (See word bank on page 25.) Ask the children to make up sentences using some of the words.
- The ‹wh› words could also be written onto a big whale shape, which can then be used as a word bank for display.

Spelling List
- Read the spelling words with the children. As a class, say the sounds in the regular words and say the letter names in the tricky words *what* and *when*. Explain that the question words *what, where, when, why, who* and *which* are all ‹wh› words. The other question words will be covered in later spelling lists.
- The last word in the list, *whenever*, is longer than the rest. The children will find this word easier to spell if they split the word into two parts, 'when' and 'ever'.

| did |
| cut |
| twin |
| whale |
| wheel |
| white |
| whisper |
| **what** |
| **when** |
| whenever |

Activity Page
- Practise the ‹wh› formation. The children write inside the outline ‹wh› on their page using the correct formation. This can be done several times using different colours.

- The children write a ‹wh› word in each whale. They draw a picture to illustrate each word.
- Encourage the children to write and colour neatly. Colouring helps the children to develop their pencil control.

Dictation
- Read the words one at a time. The children listen for the sounds in each word, and write the words on the lines.

  1. when   2. whisk
  3. whizz 4. which
  5. whale 6. whisker
  7. My cat is black and white.
  8. The rabbit has long whiskers.
  9. What did you whisper?

- Read the sentences one at a time for the children to write down.
- Remind the children that sentences start with a capital letter and end with a full stop. Point out the tricky words in the sentences.

Grammar: The Future

Aim
- To develop the children's understanding of verbs, so they know that a verb can describe the past, the present or the future.

Introduction
- Revise present and past tenses with the children.
- Call out some verbs in the present and past tenses and encourage the children to do the appropriate actions (see pages 9 and 10).
- Call out some verbs in the present tense. Make a point of choosing verbs that have a regular simple past tense, for example *to cook*, *to hop*, or *to race*. Ask the children to put these verbs into the past tense.
- Then call out some verbs in the past tense and ask the children to put them into the present tense.

Main Point
- When a verb describes an action taking place in the future, the verb root does not take a suffix, as with the past tense. Instead, the verb root has an extra word put in front of it.
- The extra word is another verb, called an *auxiliary verb*.
- The auxiliary verbs *shall* and *will* are used to describe the future.
- *Shall* can be added to the verb root for both the first person singular, *I*, and the first person plural, *we*. *Will* can be added in all persons.
- The verbs *to have* and *to jump* are conjugated below as examples of verbs in the future:
    I shall have, you will have,
    he will have, she will have, it will have,
    we shall have, you will have, they will have.
    I shall jump, you will jump,
    he will jump, she will jump, it will jump
    we shall jump, you will jump, they will jump.
- Call out some verb roots and ask the children to put them into the future.

Actions: The action for a verb that describes the future is pointing to the front.
Colour: The colour for verbs is red.

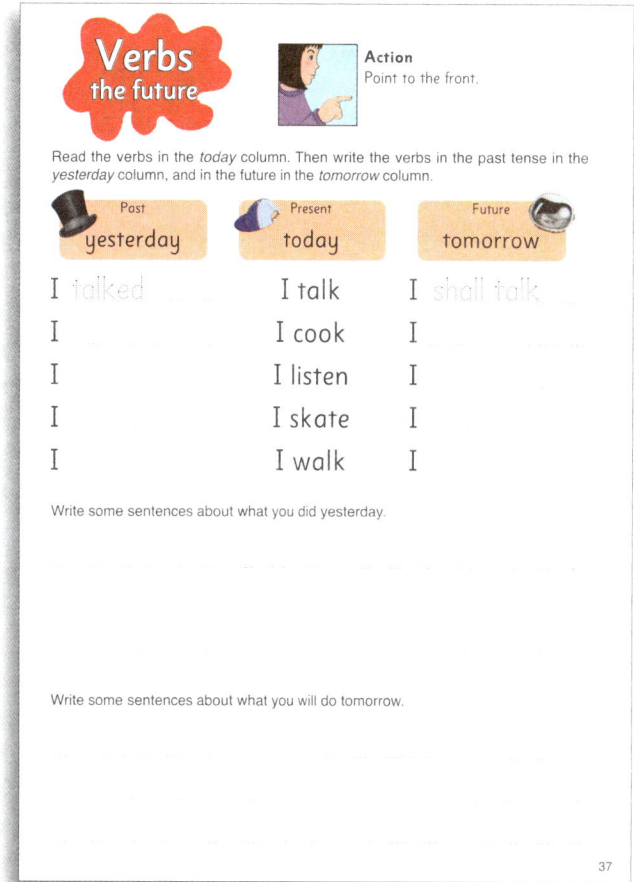

Activity Page
- The children read the list of present tense verbs in the *Today* column.
- In the *Yesterday* column, the children write the verbs in the past tense, and in the *Tomorrow* column, they write the verbs in the future.
- For the next activity, the children write some sentences about what they did yesterday and what they will do tomorrow.

Extension Activity
- Ask the children to write some more sentences about what they did yesterday.

Rounding Off
- With the children, choose a verb and conjugate it in the past, present and future.

GRAMMAR 1 PUPIL BOOK: PAGE 38

Spelling: the ‹ay› selling of the /ai/ sound

Spelling Test
- The children turn to page 76 of their *Pupil Books* and find the column labelled *Spelling Test 18*.
- In no particular order, call out the spelling words the children learnt last week:
  did, cut, twin, whale, wheel, white, whisper, what, when, whenever
- The children write these words on the lines for *Spelling Test 18*.

Revision
- Use flash cards to revise the spelling patterns taught so far, including the short and long vowels.
- Use the flash cards, or the *Tricky Word Wall Flowers*, to revise the fourth set of tricky words

Letter Sound
- Remind the children that the main ways of writing the /ai/ sound are ‹ai›, ‹a_e› and ‹ay›.
- Revise the ‹ay› spelling of the /ai/ sound. Explain that the ‹ay› spelling is often used at the end of words. The ‹y› takes the place of an ‹i›, as the letter ‹i› is 'shy' and does not like to be at the end of words.
- With the children, make a list of words that use the ‹ay› spelling and write them on the board. (See word bank on page 26.) Ask the children to make up sentences using some of the words.
- The ‹ay› words could also be written onto a big crayon shape, which can then be used as a word bank for display.

Spelling List
- Read the spelling words with the children. As a class, say the sounds in the regular words and say the letter names in the tricky words *why* and *where*. Remind the children that the question words *what, where, when, why, who* and *which* are all ‹wh› words.
- The last word in the list, *playground*, is longer than the rest. The children will find this word easier to spell if they split the word up into its two syllables, 'play' and 'ground'.

an
cat
skin
say
away
play
today
why
where
playground

Activity Page
- Practise the ‹ay› formation. The children write inside the outline ‹ay› on their page using the correct formation. This can be done several times using different colours.
- The children write an ‹ay› word in each crayon. They draw a picture to illustrate each word. Encourage the children to write and colour neatly. Colouring helps the children to develop their pencil control.

Dictation
- Read the words one at a time. The children listen for the sounds in each word, and write the words on the lines.
- Read the sentences one at a time for the children to write down.
- Remind the children that sentences start with a capital letter and end with a full stop. Point out the tricky words in the sentences.

1. hay	2. way
3. play	4. tray
5. clay	6. Sunday
7. You can all stay here.	
8. Today is hot.	
9. I made this from clay.	

Grammar: Alphabetical Order

Aim
- To develop the children's knowledge of the alphabet, and their ability to use wordbooks and dictionaries.

Introduction
- The children sit in a circle. One child says the first letter of the alphabet. Going round the circle, each child says the next letter.
- The children practise reciting the alphabet in the four groups. They hold up one finger as they say the first group, and pause, then hold up two fingers as they say the second group, and so on.
- Call out some letters. Ask the children which group each letter belongs to, for example, ‹s› is in the third (or green) group. Knowing where a letter falls in the alphabet will help the children work out where to look for it in the dictionary.

Main Point
- Look at a copy of the dictionary with the children.
- Explain to the children that words can be arranged in alphabetical order, just as letters can. Tell them that the words in a dictionary are listed in alphabetical order to make them easier to find.
- Write some words on the board. To avoid confusion at this stage, make sure each word begins with a different letter. The children look at the first letter of each word to help them arrange the words in alphabetical order.

Activity Page
- Using a different coloured pencil for each group, the children trace over the dotted lower-case letters. The first group should be red, the second yellow, the third green and the last group should be blue.
- The children then write the capital letters next to the lower-case letters.
- For the next activity, the children put the groups of letters into alphabetical order.
- Lastly, the children have to put the groups of words into alphabetical order.

Extension Activity
- Give out some dictionaries for the children to look at. They can share the books if necessary.
- Write some letters on the board. Ask the children to find words beginning with these letters in the dictionary and copy them out.
- Encourage the more able children to copy out the words' meanings as well.

Rounding Off
- Look at the activity page with the children. As a class, put the words into alphabetical order.
- Call out some letters and see if the children can find the corresponding section in the dictionary.

GRAMMAR 1 PUPIL BOOK: PAGE 40

Spelling: the ‹ea› spelling of the /ee/ sound

Spelling Test
- The children turn to page 77 of their *Pupil Books* and find the column labelled *Spelling Test 19*.
- In no particular order, call out the spelling words the children learnt last week:
  an, cat, skin, say, away, play, today, why, where, playground,
- The children write these words on the lines for *Spelling Test 19*.

Revision
- Use flash cards to revise the spelling patterns taught so far. Use the flash cards, or the *Tricky Word Wall Flowers*, to revise the fourth set of tricky words

Letter Sound
- Remind the children that the main ways of writing the /ee/ sound are ‹ee› and ‹ea›. Revise the ‹ea› spelling of the /ee/ sound.
- With the children, make a list of words that use the ‹ea› spelling and write them on the board. (See word bank on page 26.) Ask the children to make up sentences using some of the words.
- The ‹ea› words could also be written onto a big teapot shape, which can then be used as a word bank for display.

Spelling List
- Read the spelling words with the children. As a class, say the sounds in the regular words and say the letter names in the tricky words *who* and *which*. Remind the children that the question words *what, where, when, why, who* and *which* are all ‹wh› words.
- The last word in the list, *seashell*, is longer than the rest. The children will find this word easier to spell if they split the word up into its two syllables, 'sea' and 'shell'. Point out the ‹ll› spelling in *shell*.

met
web
spin
tea
heat
leaf
each
who
which
seashell

Activity Page
- Practise the ‹ea› formation. The children write inside the outline ‹ea› on their page using the correct formation.

- The children write an ‹ea› word in each teapot. They draw a picture to illustrate each word. Encourage the children to write and colour neatly. Colouring helps the children to develop their pencil control.

Dictation
- Read the words one at a time. The children listen for the sounds in each word, and write the words on the lines.

1. sea   2. peas
3. meat   4. clean
5. leaf   6. teapot
7. My room is neat and clean.
8. She took the dog to the beach.
9. He has peas in his garden.

- Read the sentences one at a time for the children to write down.
- Remind the children that sentences start with a capital letter and end with a full stop. Point out the tricky words in the sentences.

Grammar: Nouns

Aim
- To develop the children's understanding of nouns, and their ability to identify nouns in sentences.

Introduction
- Revise the parts of speech covered so far: proper and common nouns, pronouns and verbs.
- Call out some words and encourage the children to do the appropriate part-of-speech action.
- Remember that some words can function as both nouns and verbs, so the children can do both actions.

Main Point
- Look at the farm picture on the children's *Pupil Book* page.
- Ask the children to give some examples of nouns.
- Remind them that we can put the words *a*, *an* (the indefinite articles), or *the* (the definite article) before words that are common nouns.
- Write some sentences on the board. Go through the sentences, identifying the proper and common nouns with the children.
- Good example sentences include:
    The farmer drives a tractor.
    My dog goes to the vet on Monday.
- Underline the nouns in black.

Activity Page
- At the top of the page, the children write six nouns for things they can see in the picture.
- Remind the children when to use the indefinite articles *a* and *an* (see page 12).
- The children read the sentences underneath picture and underline the nouns in black.
- Explain that there can be more than one noun in a sentence.

Extension Activity
- The children write some sentences of their own about the picture and underline the nouns.
- The children could also look up their six nouns in the dictionary.

Rounding Off
- Look at the page with the children and identify the nouns as a class.

Spelling: the ‹igh› spelling of the /ie/ sound

Spelling Test
- The children turn to page 77 of their *Pupil Books* and find the column labelled *Spelling Test 20*.
- In no particular order, call out the spelling words the children learnt last week:
  met, web, spin, tea, heat, leaf, each, who, which, seaside.
- The children write these words on the lines for *Spelling Test 20*.

Revision
- Use flash cards to revise the spelling patterns taught so far, including the short and long vowels.
- Use the flash cards, or the *Tricky Word Wall Flowers*, to revise the fourth set of tricky words

Letter Sound
- Remind the children that the main ways of writing the /ie/ sound are ‹ie›, ‹i_e›, ‹igh› and ‹y›.
- Revise the ‹igh› spelling of the /ie/ sound. With the children, make a list of words that use the ‹igh› spelling and write them on the board. (See word bank on page 26.) Ask the children to make up sentences using some of the words.
- The ‹igh› words could also be written onto a big light-bulb shape, which can then be used as a word bank for display.

Spelling List
- Read the spelling words with the children. As a class, say the sounds in the regular words and say the letter names in the tricky words *any* and *many*.
- The last word in the list, *frightening*, is longer than the rest. The children will find this word easier to spell if they split the word up into its three syllables, 'frigh', 'ten' and 'ing'. It also helps the children remember the spelling if they emphasise the /e/ sound in the second syllable, pronouncing it to rhyme with *pen*.

lip
his
went
night
high
might
light
any
many
frightening

Activity Page
- Practise the ‹igh› formation. The children write inside the outline ‹igh› on their page using the correct formation.

- This can be done several times using different colours.
- The children write an ‹igh› word in each light bulb. They draw a picture to illustrate each word. Encourage the children to write and colour neatly. Colouring helps the children to develop their pencil control.

Dictation
- Read the words one at a time. The children listen for the sounds in each word, and write the words on the lines.
- Read the sentences one at a time for the children to write down.
- Remind the children that sentences start with a capital letter and end with a full stop. Point out the tricky words in the sentences.

1. high   2. sigh
3. thigh   4. sight
5. bright 6. flight
7. It was a dark night.
8. My dad had a fright.
9. There was a bright light.

GRAMMAR 1 PUPIL BOOK: PAGE 43

Grammar: Adjectives

Aim
- To introduce adjectives to the children. Adjectives are words that describe nouns.

Introduction
- Ask each child for an example of a common noun, for example *dog, hat, ball*.

Main Point
- Find, or draw, a picture of a snake. If drawing the snake, colour it in. Ask the children what the picture shows, and which part of speech the word snake is (it is a noun).
- Write the following sentence on the board:
    This is a snake.
- Underline the noun. Tell the children that this sentence does not tell us very much about the snake.
- Look at the adjective page in the *Jolly Grammar Big Book 1*, and choose one of the snakes in the picture. (If the *Jolly Grammar Big Book 1* is not available, any book with lots of illustrations of different snakes would be suitable for this activity.)
- Ask the children for a word to describe the snake, which could be added to the sentence to make it more interesting. For example, the words *long, green, spotty, sad,* or *old* could be added to the sentence.
- Choose one of the describing words and add it to the sentence on the board. Tell the children that a word that describes a noun is called an *adjective*.
- Underline the adjective in your sentence in blue, and encourage the children to do the action.
- Choose some more snakes from the picture and ask the children for adjectives to describe them. Choose one of the snakes and, with the children, find as many adjectives to describe it as possible.

Action: The action for an adjective is to touch the side of one's temple with a fist.
Colour: The colour for adjectives is blue.

Activity Page
- The children look at the picture on their page.
- They read the adjectives in the snakes' speech bubbles and colour each snake to make it fit its adjective.

- The 'long' snake needs to have its long body added, and the 'sad' snake needs a sad face.
- The children complete the phrase at the bottom of their page by writing three adjectives that could describe a snake. They colour the snake above to match these adjectives.
- Encourage the children to choose adjectives that are not found in the speech bubbles in the previous activity. They could, for example, write *scaly, shiny, frightening, slithery, happy, funny*; the list goes on.

Extension Activity
- Provide each child with a piece of paper. The children choose an adjective each and colour or decorate their piece of paper accordingly.
- Join all the pieces together, end to end, and cut out a long snake-like shape from the resulting strip. Add a head and a tail to form an 'adjectives snake'. Pin the snake up as a wall display.

Rounding Off
- Encourage some of the children to read out the phrases at the bottom of their activity page, 'a _____, _____, _____ snake'.

Spelling: the ⟨y⟩ spelling of the /ie/ sound

Spelling Test
- The children turn to page 77 of their *Pupil Books* and find the column labelled *Spelling Test 21*.
- In no particular order, call out the spelling words the children learnt last week:
  lip, his, went, night, high, might, light, any, many, frightening.
- The children write these words on the lines for *Spelling Test 21*.

Revision
- Use flash cards to revise the spelling patterns taught so far, including the short and long vowels.
- Use the flash cards, or the *Tricky Word Wall Flowers*, to revise the fourth set of tricky words

Letter Sound
- Remind the children that the main ways of writing the /ie/ sound are ⟨ie⟩, ⟨i_e⟩, ⟨igh⟩ and ⟨y⟩.
- Revise the ⟨y⟩ spelling of the /ie/ sound. With the children, make a list of words that use the ⟨y⟩ spelling and write them on the board. (See word bank on page 26.) Ask the children to make up sentences using some of the words.
- The ⟨y⟩ words could also be written onto a big frying-pan shape, which can then be used as a word bank for display.

Spelling List
- Read the spelling words with the children. As a class, say the sounds in the regular words and say the letter names in the tricky words *more* and *before*.
- The last word in the list, *myself*, is longer than the rest. The children will find this word easier to spell if they split the word up into its two syllables, 'my' and 'self'.

win
sit
stop
fry
dry
crying
sky
more
before
myself

Activity Page
- Practise the ⟨y⟩ formation. The children write inside the outline ⟨y⟩ on their page using the correct formation. This can be done several times using different colours.

- The children write a ⟨y⟩ word in each frying pan. They a draw picture to illustrate each word. Encourage the children to write and colour neatly. Colouring helps the children to develop their pencil control.

Dictation
- Read the words one at a time. The children listen for the sounds in each word, and write the words on the lines.

  1. my   2. dry
  3. pry   4. crying
  5. flying   6. trying
  7. We try not to cry.
  8. They are flying with me.
  9. He was trying to sing the song.

- Read the sentences one at a time for the children to write down.
- Remind the children that sentences start with a capital letter and end with a full stop. Point out the tricky words in the sentences.

Grammar: Adjectives

Aim
- To develop the children's ability to identify nouns and adjectives in sentences.

Introduction
- Revise common nouns. Choose a noun, for example, 'a horse'.
- Ask a child to say the noun with an adjective that describes it, for example 'a big horse'.
- Ask each child in turn to repeat what has been said and to add a new adjective to the phrase (following the rules of similar playground memory games). For example, the children could say 'a big, brown horse', 'a big, brown, kind horse', and so on.

Main Point
- Revise adjectives.
- Think of some nouns; good examples include:
    chair, jumper, dog, scarf, cat.
- Ask the children for an adjective to describe each noun.
- Use one of their suggestions to make a simple sentence, and write it on the board.
- For example:
    He had a little dog.
    She sat on the red chair.
- Underline the noun in black and the adjective in blue.

Activity Page
- The children read the adjectives written in the snake.
- Then they read the sentences in the middle of the sheet. They choose one of the adjectives to complete each sentence, and write it in the space. Alternatively, the children could use an adjective of their own choice to complete the sentence.
- The adjectives can be used more than once.

Extension Activity
- The children read the completed sentences on their *Pupil Book* page. They underline the nouns in black and the adjectives in blue.

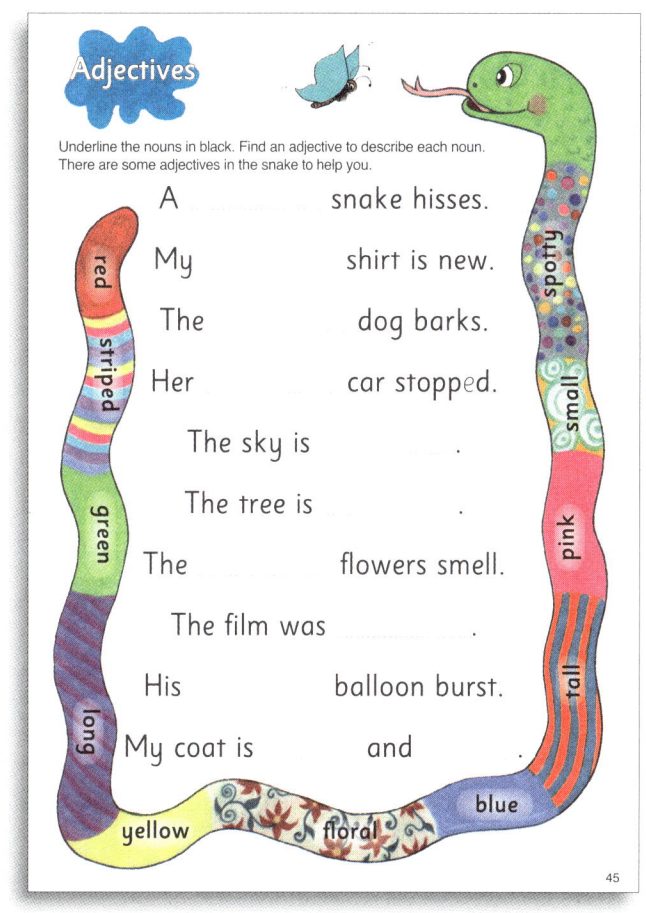

Rounding Off
- Look at the activity page with the children. Ask the children which adjectives they have chosen to use to complete each sentence.
- As long as the chosen adjectives make sense in the sentences, the children's answers are correct.

Spelling: the ‹ow› spelling of the /oa/ sound

Spelling Test
- The children turn to page 77 of their *Pupil Books* and find the column labelled *Spelling Test 22*.
- In no particular order, call out the spelling words the children learnt last week:
  win, sit, stop, fry, dry, crying, sky, more, before, myself.
- The children write these words on the lines for *Spelling Test 22*.

Revision
- Use flash cards to revise the spelling patterns taught so far, including the short and long vowels.
- Use the flash cards, or the *Tricky Word Wall Flowers*, to revise the fourth set of tricky words

Letter Sound
- Remind the children that the main ways of writing the /oa/ sound are ‹oa›, ‹o_e› and ‹ow›.
- Revise the ‹ow› spelling of the /oa/ sound.
- With the children, make a list of /oa/ words that use the ‹ow› spelling and write them on the board. (See word bank on page 26.) Ask the children to make up sentences using some of the words.
- The ‹ow› words could also be written onto a snowman shape, which can then be used as a word bank for display.

Spelling List
- Read the spelling words with the children. As a class, say the sounds in the regular words, and say the letter names in the tricky words *other* and *were*. When spelling *other*, the children can use the 'say it as it sounds' technique, pronouncing *other* to rhyme with *bother*.
- The last word in the list, *snowman*, is longer than the rest. The children will find this word easier to spell if they split the word up into its two syllables, 'snow' and 'man'.

box
job
bulb
own
grow
elbow
yellow
**other
were**
snowman

Activity Page
- Practise the ‹ow› formation. The children write inside the outline ‹ow› on their page using the correct formation.

- This can be done several times using different colours.
- The children write a ‹ow› word in each snowman. They draw a picture to illustrate each word. Encourage the children to write and colour neatly. Colouring helps the children to develop their pencil control.

Dictation
- Read the words one at a time. The children listen for the sounds in each word, and write the words on the lines.

1. own 2. low
3. mow 4. show
5. grow 6. throw
7. It has started snowing.
8. The seeds have grown well.
9. There is a show on Monday.

- Read the sentences one at a time for the children to write down.
- Remind the children that sentences start with a capital letter and end with a full stop. Point out the tricky words in the sentences.

Grammar: Final Blends

Aim
- To develop the children's ability to read and write words with final consonant blends.

Introduction
- Revise initial consonant blends.
- Hold up flash cards of initial blends for the children to read.
- Call out some of the initial consonant blends below, and ask the children to say which letters are in them.
- Initial consonant blends:

  cl bl fl gl pl sl br cr dr fr gr pr tr sc sm sn sw tw sk sp st.

Main Point
- Tell the children that not all consonant blends come at the beginning of a word. Some come at the end of a word, and are called *final blends*.
- Hold up some flash cards showing final consonant blends and ask the children to read them.
- On the board, write an example of a word using each blend. Good examples include:

  lamp, tent, sink, pond, tusk, bank, felt, milk, frost, bump, hand, vest, wind, cold, dust.
- Call out some of the final blends listed below and ask the children which letter sounds are in them.
- Final consonant blends:

  -lb -ld -lf -lk -lm -ln -lp -lt -ct -ft -nt -pt -xt -mp -nd.

Activity Page
- The children read the outlined final blends and trace inside them.
- Then they read the unfinished words and try adding a final blend to each of them. They try each final blend in turn until they find one that completes the word. For example, ‹be› and ‹-mp› makes 'bemp', which is not a real word, but ‹be› and ‹-lt› makes *belt*, which is.
- Once the children have found a blend that completes the word, they write it on the line. They illustrate their word in the box above.
- As long as the children have made real words, their answers are correct, so ‹sta› could become either *stamp* or *stand*.

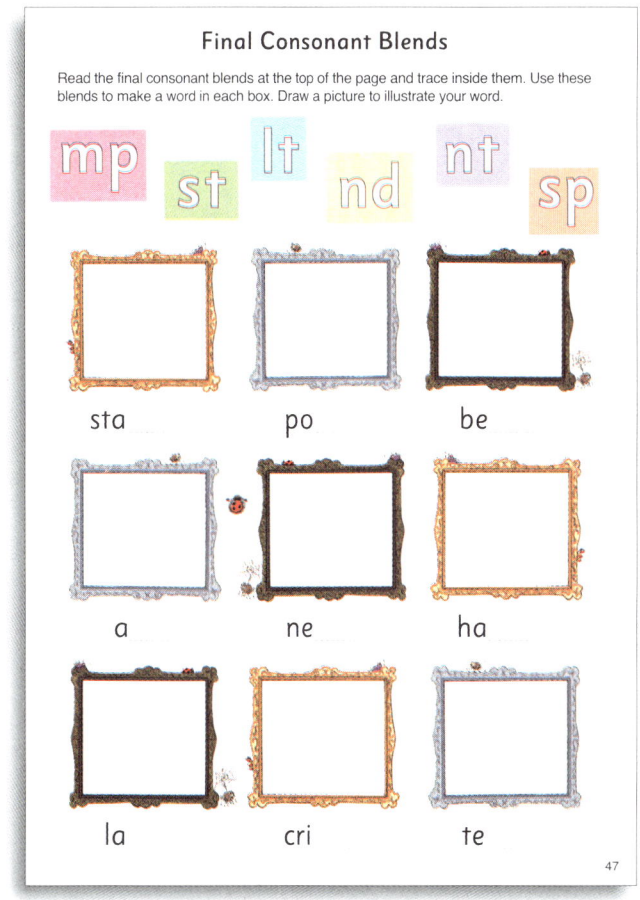

Extension Activity
- Write the unfinished words and final blends onto cards. Give the cards out to the children. They pair up the unfinished words and final blends, and see how many different words they can make.
- This exercise could be repeated with different unfinished words and final blends.
- Good examples include:

  *fa-**ct**, impa-**ct**, mi-**lk**, si-**lk**, su-**lk**, thi-**nk**, lo-**ft**, li-**ft**, shi-**ft**, si-**ft**, so-**ft**, ye-**lp**, he-**lp**, she-**lf**, e-**lf**, cre-**pt**, ke-**pt**, sle-**pt**.*

Rounding Off
- Look at the activity page with the children. Ask them to read out the words they have made. Hopefully they will have come up with lots of different words.

GRAMMAR 1 PUPIL BOOK: PAGE 48

Spelling: the ‹ew› spelling of the /ue/ sound

Spelling Test
- The children turn to page 77 of their *Pupil Books* and find the column labelled *Spelling Test 23*.
- In no particular order, call out the spelling words the children learnt last week:
  box, job, bulb, own, grow, elbow, yellow, other, were, snowman.
- The children write these words on the lines.

Revision
- Use flash cards to revise the spelling patterns taught so far, and the fourth set of tricky words

Letter Sound
- Remind the children that the main ways of writing the /ue/ sound are ‹ue›, ‹u_e› and ‹ew›.
- Explain that ‹ew› is a difficult spelling because it can make either the /ue/ sound, as in *few*, or the /oo/ sound, as in *grew*. Revise the ‹ew› spelling of the /ue/ and /oo/ sounds.
- With the children, make a list of words that use the ‹ew› spelling and write them on the board. (See word bank on page 26.) Ask the children to make up sentences using some of the words.
- The ‹ew› words could also be written onto a jewel shape, which can then be used as a word bank for display.

Spelling List
- Read the spelling words with the children. As a class, say the sounds in the regular words, and say the letter names in the tricky words *because* and *want*.
- Remind the children of the following mnemonic:
  big elephants catch ants under small elephants.
- This will help them remember how to spell *because*.
- When spelling *want*, the children can use the 'say it as it sounds' technique, pronouncing *want* to rhyme with *ant*.
- The last word in the list, *newspaper*, is longer than the rest. The children will find this word easier to spell if they split the word up into its three syllables, 'news-pa-per'.

bud
sun
held
few
flew
grew
chew
because
want
newspaper

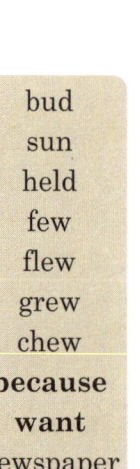

Activity Page
- Practise the ‹ew› formation. The children write inside the outline ‹ew› on their page using the correct formation. This can be done several times using different colours.
- The children write an ‹ew› word in each jewel. They draw a picture to illustrate each word. Encourage the children to write and colour neatly. Colouring helps the children to develop their pencil control.

Dictation
- Read the words one at a time. The children listen for the sounds in each word, and write the words on the lines.
- Read the sentences one at a time for the children to write down.
- Remind the children that sentences start with a capital letter and end with a full stop. Point out the tricky words in the sentences.

1. few   2. new
3. pew   4. grew
5. chew   6. drew
7. A few more can go.
8. There is my new bike.
9. He drew a newt.

Grammar: Compound Words

Aim
- To develop the children's ability to recognise compound words.

Introduction
- Revise initial and final consonant blends.
- Hold up flash cards showing the blends for the children to read. Then call out some of the blends and ask the children to identify the letters in each blend. (See page 77 for lists of initial and final consonant blends.)

Main Point
- Compound words are words made of two (or more) shorter words joined together.
- Draw some 'picture-word sums' on the board for the children to work out the compound words. For example, draw a picture of a star and a picture of a fish, and the children answer, *starfish*. Alternatively, look at the compound birds page in the *Jolly Grammar Big Book 1*. You could also show the children the *Jolly Phonics Reader, Star and Fish*.
- Other examples of 'picture-word sums' include:

    egg + cup = *eggcup*
    blue + bell = *bluebell*
    foot + ball = *football*
    tooth + brush = *toothbrush*
    black + bird = *blackbird*
    cow + boy/girl = *cowboy/cowgirl*
    sun + flower = *sunflower*
    arm + chair = *armchair*
    ear + ring = *earring*
    rain + coat = *raincoat*
    sea + shell = *seashell*
    butter + fly = *butterfly*

Activity Page
- The children read the words in the birds' wings and tails.
- Point out that the word *post* (in the first wing) has been joined to the word *man*. Explain that these two words together make the word *postman*, which is a compound word.
- Following the example, the children match up the 'tail words' and the 'wing words' to make compound words.

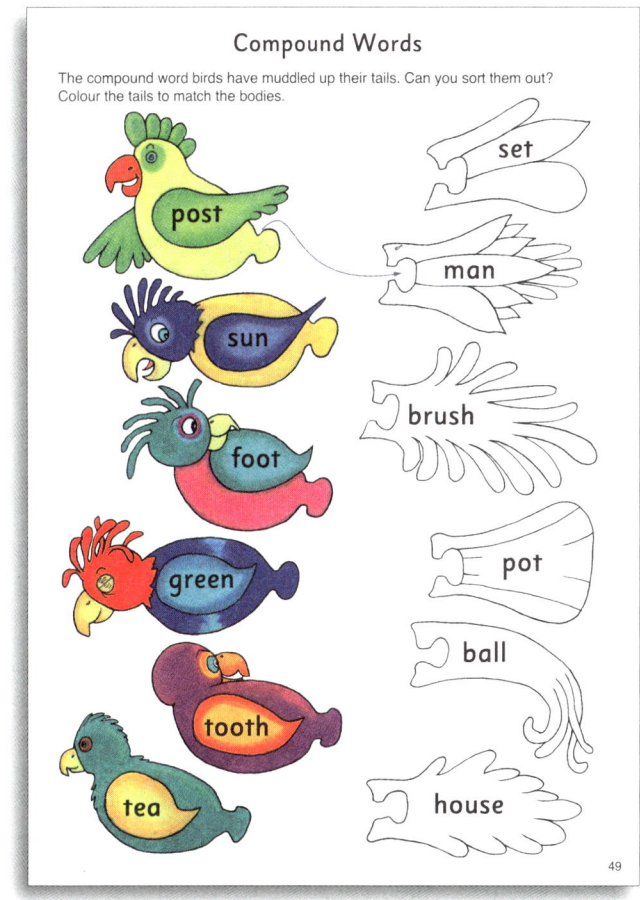

- The children could choose one of the 'wing words' and try matching each 'tail word' to it in turn until they make a compound word that makes sense. For example, *post* and *ball* makes 'postball', which is not a real word, whereas *post* and *man* makes *postman*, which is.
- When they have matched up all the words, the children can colour the birds' tails to match their bodies.

Extension Activity
- Provide the children with some more words, written on the board or on cards, and see how many compound words they can make.
- Good examples include:
  rain + bow, shoe + lace, lunch + time, lunch + box, home + work, home + time, shoe + box, letter + box, fire + work.

Rounding Off
- Look at the activity page with the children, seeing which compound words they made.

GRAMMAR 1 PUPIL BOOK: PAGE 50

Spelling: the ‹ou› spelling of the /ou/ sound

Spelling Test
- The children turn to page 77 of their *Pupil Books* and find the column labelled *Spelling Test 24*.
- In no particular order, call out the spelling words the children learnt last week:
  bud, sun, held, few, flew, grew, chew, because, want, newspaper.
- The children write these words on the lines for *Spelling Test 24*.

Revision
- Use flash cards to revise the spelling patterns taught so far. Use the flash cards, or the Tricky Word Wall Flowers, to revise the fifth set of tricky words

Letter Sound
- Remind the children that the main ways of writing the /ou/ sound are ‹ou› and ‹ow›. Revise the ‹ou› spelling of the /ou/ sound.
- With the children, make a list of words that use the ‹ou› spelling and write them on the board. (See word bank on page 26.) Ask the children to make up sentences using some of the words.
- The ‹ou› words could also be written onto a big house shape, which can then be used as a word bank for display.

Spelling List
- Read the spelling words with the children. As a class, say the sounds in the regular words, and say the letter names in the tricky words *saw* and *put*.
- The last word in the list, *outside*, is a compound word. The children will find this word easier to spell if they split the word up into the two shorter words, 'out' and 'side'.

| bat |
| pet |
| self |
| out |
| our |
| round |
| mouth |
| **saw** |
| **put** |
| outside |

Activity Page
- Practise the ‹ou› formation. The children write inside the outline ‹ou› on their page using the correct formation. This can be done several times using different colours.
- The children write an ‹ou› word in each house. They draw a picture to illustrate each word.

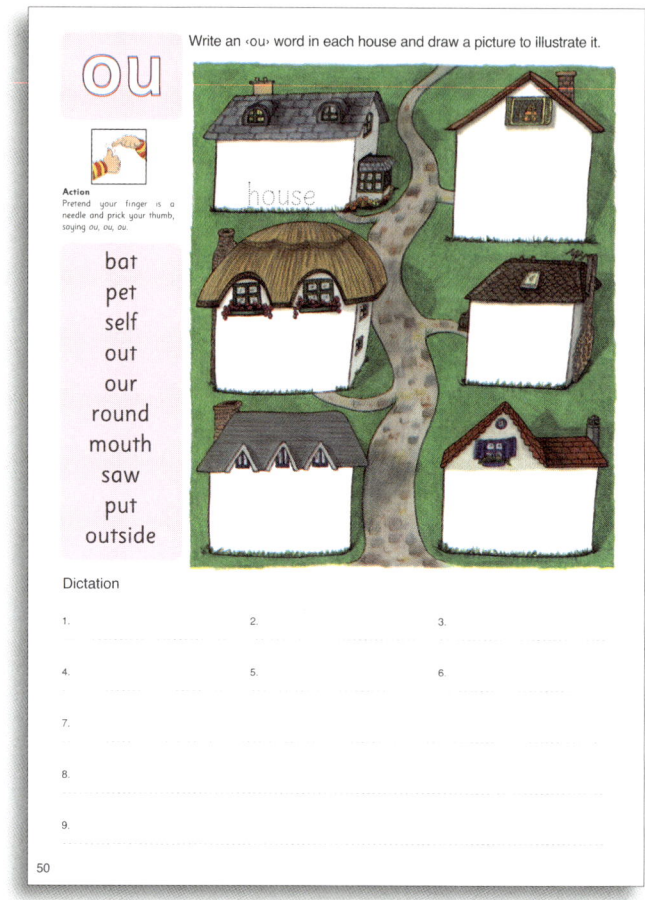

- Encourage the children to write and colour neatly. Colouring helps the children to develop their pencil control.

Dictation
- Read the words one at a time. The children listen for the sounds in each word, and write the words on the lines.

  1. our
  2. loud
  3. south
  4. flour
  5. found
  6. round
  7. The hoop is round.
  8. Dad needs some flour to make a cake.
  9. He counted to fifty.

- Read the sentences one at a time for the children to write down.
- Remind the children that sentences start with a capital letter and end with a full stop. Point out the tricky words in the sentences.

Grammar: Alphabetical Order

Aim
- To develop the children's knowledge of the alphabet, and their ability to put words into alphabetical order.

Introduction
- The children sit in a circle, and one child says the first letter of the alphabet. Go round the circle with each child saying the next letter.
- The children practise saying the alphabet, pausing between each of the four groups. They hold up one finger as they say the first group of letters, then hold up two fingers as they say the second, and so on.

Main Point
- Write some words on the board. At this stage, try to ensure that each word begins with a different letter. With the children's help, put the words into alphabetical order.
- Write a word on the board that the children will recognise, even when it is deliberately mis-spelt, for example, 'mumy'.
- Ask the children if the word is spelt correctly. Tell the children that if they are not sure whether a spelling is correct, they can check it with a dictionary. Look up the word *mummy* in the dictionary and read out the letters, asking the children to check the spelling on the board.
- Explain that if they do not know how a word is spelt, but can sound out the first few letters, then they will probably be able to find it in a dictionary.

Activity Page
- The children read each group of words. Then they copy out the words in alphabetical order on the lines underneath.
- For the next activity, the children look at the pictures at the bottom of the sheet, and try writing the word for each picture. Once they have finished writing, they can check their spelling in a dictionary. Although the children may not know how to spell the word *television*, they will probably be able to sound out the first few letters.

- If these words are not in the children's dictionaries, the exercise could be treated as a whole-class activity, using a dictionary that does contain the words.

Extension Activity
- Draw some pictures on the board, or find some pictures of objects and hold them up. The children try to write the words for each picture and then check their spellings in a dictionary.

Rounding Off
- Look at the activity page with the children.
- Call out some letters and see how quickly the children can find the corresponding section in their dictionaries.

Spelling: the ‹ow› spelling of the /ou/ sound

Spelling Test
- The children turn to page 78 of their *Pupil Books* and find the column labelled *Spelling Test 25*.
- In no particular order, call out the spelling words the children learnt last week:
  bat, pet, self, out, our, round, mouth, saw, put, outside.
- The children write these words on the lines for *Spelling Test 25*.

Revision
- Use flash cards to revise the spelling patterns taught so far, and the fifth set of tricky words.

Letter Sound
- Remind the children that the main ways of writing the /ou/ sound are ‹ou› and ‹ow›. Revise the ‹ow› spelling of the /ou/ sound.
- With the children, make a list of words that use the ‹ow› spelling of the /ou/ sound and write them on the board. (See word bank on page 26.) Ask the children to make up sentences using some of the words.
- The ‹ow› words could also be written onto a big owl shape, which can then be used as a word bank for display.

Spelling List

| big |
| fox |
| milk |
| how |
| owl |
| brown |
| town |
| **could** |
| **should** |
| flowerpot |

- Read the spelling words with the children. As a class, say the sounds in the regular words, and say the letter names in the tricky words *could* and *should*.
- Introduce the mnemonic **o u** lucky **d**uck; this helps the children remember how to spell the endings of these two words.
- The last word in the list, *flowerpot*, is a compound word. The children will find this word easier to spell if they split the word up into the two shorter words, 'flower' and 'pot'.

Activity Page
- Practise the ‹ow› formation. The children write inside the outline ‹ow› on their page using the correct formation.

- The children write an ‹ow› word in each owl. They draw a picture to illustrate each word.
- Encourage the children to write and colour neatly. Colouring helps the children to develop their pencil control.

Dictation
- Read the words one at a time. The children listen for the sounds in each word, and write the words on the lines.

1. cow   2. now
3. clown   4. howl
5. crowd   6. powder
7. Come down here.
8. They went to town on the bus.
9. She had a quick shower.

- Read the sentences one at a time for the children to write down.
- Remind the children that sentences start with a capital letter and end with a full stop. Point out the tricky words in the sentences.

Grammar: Verbs

Aim
- To develop the children's understanding of verbs, and their ability to identify verbs in sentences.

Introduction
- Revise the parts of speech covered so far: proper and common nouns, pronouns, verbs and adjectives.
- If the *Jolly Grammar Big Book 1* is available, use the parts of speech pages to help prompt the children.
- Call out some words and encourage the children to do the appropriate actions. Remember that some words can function as both nouns and verbs, so the children can do both actions.

Main Point
- Revise verbs. Look at the seaside picture on the children's *Pupil Book* page.
- Ask the children to give some examples of verbs. Remind them that if we can put the word *to* in front of a word, then it is probably a verb.
- Write some sentences on the board. Read through the sentences, finding the verbs with the children.
- Good examples of sentences include:
    The girls jump in the water.
    The dog chews his bone.
- Underline the verbs in red.

Activity Page
- The children look at the seaside picture and write six verbs for the actions they can see.
- The children read the sentences underneath the picture, and underline the verbs in red.
- Point out that there can be more than one verb in a sentence.

Extension Activity
- The children write some sentences of their own about the picture, and underline the verbs in red.
- The children could also look up their six verbs in the dictionary.

Rounding Off
- Look at the activity sheet with the children and encourage them to identify the verbs.

GRAMMAR 1 PUPIL BOOK: PAGE 54

Spelling: the ‹oi› spelling of the /oi/ sound

Spelling Test
- The children turn to page 78 of their *Pupil Books* and find the column labelled *Spelling Test 26*.
- In no particular order, call out the spelling words the children learnt last week:
  big, fox, milk, how, owl, brown, town, could, should, flowerpot
- The children write these words on the lines for *Spelling Test 26*.

Revision
- Use flash cards to revise the spelling patterns taught so far.
- Use the flash cards, or the *Tricky Word Wall Flowers*, to revise the fifth set of tricky words

Letter Sound
- Remind the children that the main ways of writing the /oi/ sound are ‹oi› and ‹oy›. Revise the ‹oi› spelling of the /oi/ sound.
- With the children, make a list of words that use the ‹oi› spelling of the /oi/ sound and write them on the board. (See word bank on page 26.) Ask the children to make up sentences using some of the words.
- The ‹oi› words could also be written onto a big oil can shape, which can then be used as a word bank for display.

Spelling List
- Read the spelling words with the children. As a class, say the sounds in the regular words, and say the letter names in the tricky words *would* and *right*.
- Remind the children of the mnemonic **o u lucky d**uck, which will help them remember how to spell *would*.
- *Right* is not really a tricky word, but the children need to remember that the /ie/ sound spelt ‹igh›.
- The last word in the list, *boiling*, is longer than the rest. The children will find this word easier to spell if they split the word up into its two syllables, 'boil' and 'ing'.

bug
had
film
oil
coin
noisy
toil
would
right
boiling

Activity Page
- Practise the ‹oi› formation. The children write inside the outline ‹oi› on their page using the correct formation. This can be done several times using different colours.
- The children write an ‹oi› word in each oil can. They draw pictures to illustrate each word. Encourage the children to write and colour neatly. Colouring helps the children to develop their pencil control.

Dictation
- Read the words one at a time. The children listen for the sounds in each word, and write the words on the lines.
- Read the sentences one at a time for the children to write down. Remind the children that sentences start with a capital letter and end with a full stop. Point any tricky words.

1. boil
2. join
3. soil
4. joint
5. foil
6. spoil
7. It was a noisy car.
8. They are pointing at me.
9. The snake coils around the tree.

Grammar: Adverbs

Aim
- To introduce adverbs to the children. Adverbs are words that describe verbs.

Introduction
- Revise verbs. With the children, look at a picture that shows lots of things happening.
- Ask the children to identify some of the verbs that are illustrated. Write some of the suggested verbs on the board.
- Underline the verbs in red.

Main Point
- Remind the children that we use a particular type of word, called an *adjective*, to describe a noun.
- Then explain that there is another type of word, called an *adverb*, that we can use to describe a verb.
- There is a page in the *Jolly Grammar Big Book 1* that will help introduce adverbs.
- With the children, think of some suitable adverbs that could be used to describe the verbs on the board.
- Write an adverb in front of each of the verbs on the written board.
- Underline the adverbs in orange.

Action: The action for an adverb is to bang one fist on top of the other.
Colour: The colour for adverbs is orange.

Activity Page
- The children read the adverbs at the top of their *Pupil Book* page. Then they read the unfinished sentence underneath each picture. They decide which adverb could be used to complete each sentence, and copy it out on the line provided.

Extension Activity
- Write some verbs on the board and ask the children to think of an adverb to describe each one.
- Good examples of verbs to choose include: *speak, swim, sing, build, clean, paint, drive, play.*

Rounding Off
- Look at the activity page with the children. As long as their chosen adverbs make sense in the sentences, the children's answers are correct.

Spelling: the ‹oy› spelling of the /oi/ sound

Spelling Test
- The children turn to page 78 of their *Pupil Books* and find the column labelled *Spelling Test 27*.
- In no particular order, call out the spelling words the children learnt last week:
  bug, had, film, oil, coin, noisy, toilet, would, right, boiling.
- The children write these words on the lines for *Spelling Test 27*.

Revision
- Use flash cards to revise the spelling patterns taught so far and the fifth set of tricky words

Letter Sound
- Remind the children that the main ways of writing the /oi/ sound are ‹oi› and ‹oy›. Revise the ‹oy› spelling of the /oi/ sound.
- Explain that the ‹oy› spelling is often used at the end of words. The ‹y› takes the place of an ‹i›, as the letter ‹i› is 'shy' and does not like to be at the end of words.
- With the children, make a list of words that use the ‹oy› spelling of the /oi/ sound and write them on the board. Ask the children to make up sentences using some of the words.
- The ‹oi› words could also be written onto a big toy shape, which can then be used as a word bank for display.
- There are not many ‹oy› words. However, a few suitable examples are included in the word bank on page 26.

Spelling List
- Read the spelling words with the children. As a class, say the sounds in the regular words, and say the letter names in the tricky words *two* and *four*.
- The last word in the list, *destroy*, is longer than the rest. The children will find this word easier to spell if they split the word up into its two syllables, 'des' and 'troy'.

jet
dig
help
boy
toy
enjoy
annoy
two
four
destroy

Activity Page
- Practise the ‹oy› formation. The children write inside the outline ‹oy› on their page using the correct formation. This can be done several times using different colours.
- The children write an ‹oy› word in each toy shape. They draw pictures to illustrate each word. Encourage the children to write and colour neatly. Colouring helps the children to develop their pencil control.

Dictation
- Read the words one at a time. The children listen for the sounds in each word, and write the words on the lines.

  1. boy   2. toy
  3. joy   4. enjoy
  5. royal 6. annoy
  7. They enjoyed the trip.
  8. The fly was annoying the boy.
  9. His toy car had a crash.

- Read the sentences one at a time for the children to write down. Remind the children that sentences start with a capital letter and end with a full stop. Point out the tricky words in the sentences.

Grammar: Adverbs

Aim
- To develop the children's understanding of adverbs.

Introduction
- Revise verbs.
- Discuss recent outings with the children. They might like to talk about a recent holiday, or a school trip.
- Ask the children where they think Inky, Snake and Bee might like to go on an outing; for example to the park, or the seaside. Think of things Inky, Snake and Bee might like to do whilst on their outing, for example, climb a tree, or build a sand castle.
- Make a list of these activities, and write them on the board.

Main Point
- Revise adverbs.
- With the children, think of some adverbs that could be used to describe the verbs listed on the board.

Activity Page
- Read the title of the story with the children, *Bee's Busy Day*.
- Explain that the word *busy* is a difficult word to read because the /i/-/z/ sound in the middle is written with a ‹u› and an ‹s›.
- The children read story in the beehive, pausing at the gaps. Then they read the adverbs at the top of their page, and decide which adverb could be used to fill each gap. They write the adverbs in the appropriate gaps.
- The story could be completed as it is shown below. However, as long as the adverbs used are appropriate in the context, the children should get a tick.

Extension Activity
- The children write about, or draw a picture of, something they think Inky, Snake and Bee might do on their day out.

Rounding Off
- Look at the activity page with the children. As long as the children's chosen adverbs make sense in the sentences, their answers are correct.
- Ask the children where they think Inky, Snake and Bee went on their outing.

Bee woke up <u>suddenly</u>, and traipsed <u>slowly</u> down the hive to have breakfast. She buzzed <u>loudly</u> as she flew to the farm. She <u>soon</u> collected as much pollen as she could, and flew <u>quickly</u> back to the hive. She smiled <u>happily</u> to herself. Bee, and her friends Inky and Snake, had planned a day out.

Spelling: the ‹or› spelling of the /or/ sound

Spelling Test
- The children turn to page 78 of their *Pupil Books* and find the column labelled *Spelling Test 28*.
- In no particular order, call out the spelling words the children learnt last week:
  jet, dig, help, boy, toy, enjoy, annoy, two, four, destroy.
- The children write these words on the lines for *Spelling Test 28*.

Revision
- Use flash cards to revise the spelling patterns taught so far.
- Use the flash cards, or the *Tricky Word Wall Flowers*, to revise the fifth set of tricky words

Letter Sound
- Revise the ‹or› spelling of the /or/ sound.
- With the children, make a list of words that use the ‹or› spelling and write them on the board. (See word bank on page 26.) Ask the children to make up sentences using some of the words.
- The ‹or› words could also be written onto a big horse shape, which can then be used as a word bank for display.

Spelling List
- Read the spelling words with the children. As a class, say the sounds in the regular words, and say the letter names in the tricky words *goes* and *does*.
- The last word in the list, *morning*, is longer than the rest. The children will find this word easier to spell if they split the word up into its two syllables, 'morn' and 'ing'.

got
bun
belt
fork
storm
horse
forty
goes
does
morning

Activity Page
- Practise the ‹or› formation. The children write inside the outline ‹or› on their page using the correct formation. This can be done several times using different colours.
- The children write an ‹or› word in each horse. They draw pictures to illustrate each word.
- Encourage the children to write and colour neatly. Colouring helps the children to develop their pencil control.

Dictation
- Read the words one at a time. The children listen for the sounds in each word, and write the words on the lines.

1. corn   2. sort
3. worn   4. torch
5. for   6. sport
7. We cut the corn.
8. She is good at sports.
9. There was a storm this morning.

- Read the sentences one at a time for the children to write down.
- Remind the children that sentences start with a capital letter and end with a full stop. Point out the tricky words in the sentences.

Grammar: Plurals

Aim
- To develop the children's understanding of singular and plural.
- The children are introduced to the idea that, if a word ends in ‹sh›, ‹ch›, ‹s› or ‹x›, the plural is made by adding ‹es›.

Introduction
- Revise singular and plural.
- Write some sentences on the board.
- Good example sentences include:
    The dog barked loudly.
    The cat walked slowly.
- With the children, identify the different parts of speech, and underline them in the appropriate colours.
- Ask the children to make the nouns plural by adding a letter ‹s›.

Main Point
- Explain to the children that, if a word ends in ‹sh›, ‹ch›, ‹s› or ‹x›, then the plural is made by adding ‹es›.
- Examples of words that are made plural with the ‹es› suffix include:
wish, church, dress, box, dish, bunch, kiss, fox, crash, catch, pass, six, brush, ditch, class, fix.

Activity Page
- The children write inside the outlined letters in the left-hand column on their page.
- The children read the first spelling pattern, ‹sh›, and think of a noun that ends with this spelling pattern; examples include *dish*, *wish* and *brush*.
- In the middle column on their page, they trace over the word *brush*.
- In the final column, the children have to make their noun plural. They do this by adding ‹es› to the end of the noun. The children trace over the word *brushes*.
- The children complete their page, writing the singular nouns in the middle column and the plural nouns in the right-hand column.
- Once they have finished writing, the children can draw a picture illustrating each of their words.
- Remind the children that they must draw more than one item when illustrating a plural word.

Extension Activity
- Think of some sentences that have nouns in the singular, and write them on the board. Ask the children to rewrite the sentences with plural nouns. The sentences should include some nouns that are made plural by adding ‹es›, and some nouns that are made plural by adding ‹s›.
- Alternatively the children could think of as many words as they can that end with ‹sh›, ‹ch›, ‹s› or ‹x›, and write them in the singular and the plural.

Rounding Off
- Call out some nouns. Ensure that some of the nouns in the list are made plural with an ‹es› suffix, and some with an ‹s› suffix.
- The children listen carefully to each word, and say which letter(s) should be added.

Spelling: the ‹al› spelling of the /or/ sound

Spelling Test
- The children turn to page 78 of their *Pupil Books* and find the column labelled *Spelling Test 29*.
- In no particular order, call out the spelling words the children learnt last week:
  got, bun, belt, fork, storm, horse, forty, goes, does, morning.
- The children write these words on the lines for *Spelling Test 29*.

Revision
- Use flash cards to revise the spelling patterns taught so far, and the fifth set of tricky words

Letter Sound
- Revise the ‹or› spelling of the /or/ sound. Explain to the children that the /or/ sound can also be written ‹al›.
- Remind the children that the ‹al› in the tricky word *all* makes an /or/ sound. Ask the children if they can think of any other words in which ‹al› makes an /or/ sound.
- With the children, make a list of words that use the ‹al› spelling and write them on the board. (See word bank on page 26.) Ask the children to make up sentences using some of the words.
- The ‹al› words could also be written onto a big 'talk bubble' shape, which can then be used as a word bank for display.

Spelling List
- Read the spelling words with the children. As a class, say the sounds in the regular words, and say the letter names in the tricky words *made* and *their*. *Made* is not really a tricky word, but the children need to remember that the /ai/ sound is spelt ‹a_e›.
- The last word in the list, *beanstalk*, is a compound word. The children will find this word easier to spell if they split the word up into its two syllables, 'bean' and 'stalk'.

bad
vet
fact
all
talk
walk
small
made
their
beanstalk

Activity Page
- Practise the ‹al› formation. The children write inside the outline ‹al› on their page using the correct formation. This can be done several times using different colours.
- The children write an ‹al› word in each speech bubble. They draw pictures to illustrate each word. Encourage the children to write and colour neatly. Colouring helps the children to develop their pencil control.

Dictation
- Read the words one at a time. The children listen for the sounds in each word, and write the words on the lines.

1. also   2. talk
3. always 4. falling
5. ball   6. wall
7. They took a short walk.
8. He always hits the ball.
9. The beanstalk grew tall.

- Read the sentences one at a time for the children to write down.
- Remind the children that sentences start with a capital letter and end with a full stop. Point out the tricky words in the sentences.

Grammar: Antonyms

Aim
- To introduce antonyms to the children. An *antonym* is another word for an *opposite*.

Introduction
- Give a few examples of pairs of antonyms.
- Good examples include:
  - *big* and *small*,
  - *dark* and *light*,
  - *up* and *down*,
  - *night* and *day*.
- Call out some words and ask the children to respond with the antonyms. See if the children can suggest any antonym pairs of their own.

Main Point
- Copy the short passage, below, onto the board and read it with the children.

> *A tall man drove backwards out of his garage and on to a rough road. At the roundabout he turned right. It was a dark, wet night. He made a quick turn at a small bend in the road and hit a low wall. The car went over the wall and stopped.*

- With the children, identify all the words that have antonyms. Remove these words from the story and write the antonyms in their place.
- Read the story again, and see if it still makes sense.

Activity Page
- The children read the words on their *Pupil Book* page. They write the antonym for each word on the line opposite.
- They illustrate each antonym in the space above.

Extension Activity
- Write some jumbled-up antonym pairs on the board. The children identify the pairs, and copy them out.
- Alternatively, the antonyms pairs could be written onto cards for the children to match up.

- Good examples of antonym pairs include:
  - *backwards / forwards*,   *little / big*,
  - *easy / difficult*,   *right / left*,
  - *good / bad*,   *long / short*,
  - *rough / smooth*,   *wet / dry*,
  - *sharp / blunt*,   *fat / thin*,
  - *new / old*,   *liquid / solid*,
  - *slow / fast*,   *small / large*,
  - *right / wrong*,   *over / under*,
  - *high / low*,   *dark / light*,

Rounding Off
- Call out some phrases, or sentences, which include words with antonyms.
- Ask the children to replace these words with their antonyms.
- For example, *a big dog* could expect the response *a small dog*; *he walked slowly* becomes *he walked quickly*; *an easy sum* becomes *a hard sum*, and so on.

Spelling: ‹nk› saying /ng-k/

Spelling Test
- The children turn to page 78 of their *Pupil Books* and find the column labelled *Spelling Test 30*.
- In no particular order, call out the spelling words the children learnt last week:
  bad, vet, fact, all, talk, walk, small, made, their, beanstalk.
- The children write these words on the lines for *Spelling Test 30*.

Revision
- Use flash cards to revise the spelling patterns taught so far.
- Use the flash cards, or the *Tricky Word Wall Flowers*, to revise the sixth set of tricky words

Letter Sound
- Introduce the ‹nk› spelling for the combined sounds /ng/ and /k/. When these two sounds come together, they are almost always written ‹nk›, so it is an important spelling pattern to learn.
- With the children, make a list of words that use the ‹nk› spelling and write them on the board. (See word bank on page 26.) Ask the children to make up sentences using some of the words.
- The ‹nk› words could also be written onto a big drink shape, which can then be used as a word bank for display.

Spelling List
- Read the spelling words with the children. As a class, say the sounds in the regular words, and say the letter names in the tricky words *once* and *upon*.
- The last word in the list, *winking*, is longer than the rest. The children will find this word easier to spell if they split the word up into its two syllables, 'wink' and 'ing'.

fin
sob
left
sink
pink
drink
think
once
upon
winking

Activity Page
- Practise the joined ‹nk› formation. The children write inside the outline ‹nk› on their page using the correct formation. This can be done several times using different colours.

- The children write an ‹nk› word in each drink. They draw pictures to illustrate each word. Encourage the children to write and colour neatly. Colouring helps the children to develop their pencil control.

Dictation
- Read the words one at a time. The children listen for the sounds in each word, and write the words on the lines.

1. ink	2. rink
3. blink	4. trunk
5. drank	6. shrink
7. The pink bird blinks.	
8. What would you like to drink?	
9. I sleep in the top bunk.	

- Read the sentences one at a time for the children to write down.
- Remind the children that sentences start with a capital letter and end with a full stop. Point out the tricky words in the sentences.

Grammar: Using a Dictionary

Aim
- To develop the children's knowledge of the alphabet, and their ability to use wordbooks and dictionaries.

Introduction
- The children sit in a circle and say the letters of the alphabet in turn. Then they practise reciting the alphabet, pausing between each of the four groups. They hold up one finger as they say the first group of letters, then hold up two fingers as they say the second group, and so on.
- Call out some letters. Ask the children which group each letter belongs to; for example ‹s› is in the third (or green) group of letters. Knowing where a letter is in the alphabet will help the children to work out where to look for it in the dictionary.
- Call out a letter and ask the children to say which letter comes before it, and which letter comes after it in the alphabet. Repeat this activity with other letters.

Main Point
- Explain that the children can use a dictionary to help them when they are not sure how a word is spelt. Tell the children that they will need to sound out the first few letters of the word, and find the appropriate section of the dictionary, before they can look for the word. If they have already written a word, but decide that it looks wrong, the children can check the word's spelling by looking it up in the dictionary.
- Write a few words on the board, mis-spelling some of them. Good examples include 'leter', 'animal', and 'biskit'.
- Ensure that all the words are included in the children's dictionaries.
- Ask the children whether they think the words are spelt correctly. Look the words up in a dictionary and correct them with the children.

Activity Page
- Underneath each picture on the children's *Pupil Book* page there are two possible spellings. The children read both spellings, then look up the word in the dictionary and tick the correct spelling.
- For the next activity, the children read the three mis-spelt words. They look up each of these words in the dictionary and correct the spellings. They might like to use coloured pencils to make their corrections clear.
- Lastly, the children look up the two words at the bottom of their page, and copy out the meanings given in their dictionaries. Make sure that all the words on the *Pupil Book* page are included in the dictionaries used by the children.

Extension Activity
- Write some more words on the board and ask the children to find out what they mean. The words could be related to a topic the children are currently studying.

Rounding Off
- Look at the activity page with the children, checking the spellings and the meanings of the words.

GRAMMAR 1 PUPIL BOOK: PAGE 64

Spelling: the ‹er› spelling of the /er/ sound

Spelling Test
- The children turn to page 79 of their *Pupil Books* and find the column labelled *Spelling Test 31*.
- In no particular order, call out the spelling words the children learnt last week:
  fin, sob, left, sink, pink, drink, thank, once, upon, winking.
- The children write these words on the lines for *Spelling Test 31*.

Revision
- Use flash cards to revise the spelling patterns taught so far, and the sixth set of tricky words

Letter Sound
- Remind the children that the main ways of writing the /er/ sound are ‹er›, ‹ir› and ‹ur›. Revise the ‹er› spelling of the /er/ sound.
- Point out that the ‹er› spelling often comes at the end of words.
- With the children, make a list of words that use the ‹er› spelling of the /er/ sound and write them on the board. (See word bank on page 26.) Ask the children to make up sentences using some of the words. The ‹er› words could also be written onto a big gingerbread shape, which can then be used as a word bank for display.

Spelling List
- Read the spelling words with the children. As a class, say the sounds in the regular words, and say the letter names in the tricky words *always* and *also*.
- Explain to the children that when *all* is part of a compound word, it loses the second ‹l›.
- The last word in the list, *woodpecker*, is also a compound word. The children will find this word easier to spell if they split the word up into its three syllables, 'wood', 'peck' and 'er'.

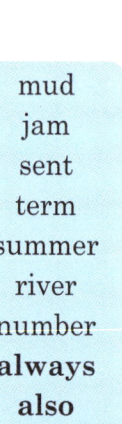

mud
jam
sent
term
summer
river
number
always
also
woodpecker

- The children write an ‹er› word in each gingerbread biscuit. They draw pictures to illustrate each word. Encourage the children to write and colour neatly. Colouring helps the children to develop their pencil control.

Dictation
- Read the words one at a time. The children listen for the sounds in each word, and write the words on the lines.

  1. herd   2. fern
  3. term   4. never
  5. winter 6. silver
  7. I grew some ferns.
  8. Her ring is made of silver.
  9. There are fish in the river.

- Read the sentences one at a time for the children to write down.
- Remind the children that sentences start with a capital letter and end with a full stop. Point out the tricky words in the sentences.

Activity Page
- Practise the joined ‹er› formation. The children write inside the outline ‹er› on their page using the correct formation.

Grammar: Speech Marks

Aim
- To develop the children's knowledge of punctuation and to introduce speech marks.

Introduction
- Find a comic or book that uses speech bubbles. Ask the children what the speech bubbles are for. Read some of the text in the bubbles.
- Draw a speech bubble on the board. Next to the speech bubble, draw an animal or write its name. Ask the children what noise the animal makes. Write this sound in the speech bubble.
- Ask the children to think of some more animals and the sounds that they make. Write some of these sounds in speech bubbles on the board.

Main Point
- Show the children a page of text that has speech marks in it. Point out the speech marks, and see if the children can say why they are there.
- Point out that the first word after the opening speech marks usually has a capital letter.
- Explain that the speech marks are used before and after any words that are spoken. The words that come out of our mouths are called *speech*, and it is only these words that go between the speech marks.
- It may be helpful to liken the speech marks to a *66* before the speech, and a *99* after it. This can help the children to remember how to write the speech marks correctly.
- Read aloud from the book; encourage the children to look out for the speech marks and read the spoken words themselves.
- There is a page in the *Jolly Grammar Big Book 1* that will help you introduce speech marks.

Activity Page
- The children write inside the outlined speech marks at the top of the page.
- They write the noise each animal makes in the speech bubbles. For example, the snake would say 'Hiss'. Then they write the noise in the box underneath the animal. Remind the children to begin each animal noise with a capital letter.

- In the first two examples, the speech marks are provided in outline, and the children have to trace inside them. For the remaining animals the children should write the speech marks themselves in the circles provided.

Extension Activity
- Write some sentences on the board. The children copy the sentences and add in the speech marks.
- Good example sentences include:
    Woof, woof said the dog.
    Meow said the cat.
    Roar said the lion.

Rounding Off
- Look at the activity page with the children. Ask them what sounds each animal might make.
- Read through any sentences on the board and identify where the speech marks should go.

GRAMMAR 1 PUPIL BOOK: PAGE 66

Spelling: the ‹ir› spelling of the /er/ sound

Spelling Test
- The children turn to page 79 of their *Pupil Books* and find the column labelled *Spelling Test 32*.
- In no particular order, call out the spelling words the children learnt last week:
  mud, jam, sent, term, summer, river, number, always, also, woodpecker
- The children write these words on the lines for *Spelling Test 32*.

Revision
- Use flash cards to revise the spelling patterns taught so far, and the sixth set of tricky words

Letter Sound
- Remind the children that the main ways of writing the /er/ sound are ‹er›, ‹ir› and ‹ur›. Revise the ‹ir› spelling of the / er / sound.
- With the children, make a list of words that use the ‹ir› spelling of the /er/ sound and write them on the board. (See word bank on page 26.) Ask the children to make up sentences using some of the words. Tell the children that an /er/ sound in a number word will probably be spelt ‹ir›. For example in the words *first*, *third*, *thirteen* and *thirty* the /er/ sound is written ‹ir›.
- The ‹ir› words could also be written onto a big bird shape, which can then be used as a word bank for display.

Spelling List
- Read the spelling words with the children. As a class, say the sounds in the regular words, and say the letter names in the tricky words *of* and *eight*. Remind the children to write *of* with an ‹f›, even though it has a /v/ sound at the end.
- The last word in the list, *birthday*, is a compound word. The children will find this word easier to spell if they split the word up into its two syllables, 'birth' and 'day'. Encourage the children to emphasise the /th/ sound at the end of *birth*.

yet
hid
wept
skirt
girl
shirt
first
of
eight
birthday

Activity Page
- Practise the joined ‹ir› formation. The children write inside the outline ‹ir› on their page using the correct formation. This can be done several times using different colours.
- The children write an ‹ir› word in each bird. They draw pictures to illustrate each word. Encourage the children to write and colour neatly. Colouring helps the children to develop their pencil control.

Dictation
- Read the words one at a time. The children listen for the sounds in each word, and write the words on the lines.

  1. dirt 2. stir
  3. sir 4. third
  5. thirty 6. bird
  7. The girl is thirsty.
  8. When is your birthday?
  9. I have a green skirt and red shirt.

- Read the sentences one at a time for the children to write down. Remind the children that sentences start with a capital letter and end with a full stop. Point out the tricky words in the sentences.

Grammar: Word Web Synonyms

Aim
- To encourage the children to think about the words they choose to use in their writing.

Introduction
- Explain that some words can have the same, or similar, meanings. For example, *happy*, *jolly*, *cheerful* and *merry* all have similar meanings.
- Ask the children if they can think of any more words that mean *happy*. Good examples include: *pleased*, *thrilled*, *delighted*, *content*, *grinning*, *glad*, *cheery*, *beaming*, *chirpy*.
- Ask the children if they can think of any other words that have similar meanings.
- The following words have a large number of synonyms:
sad, *hot*, *dirty*, *small*, *big*, *hurry*, *horrible*.
- The children could also be shown a thesaurus. Explain that a thesaurus is a special book, which lists words with similar meanings.

Main Point
- Tell the children that they can make their writing more interesting by thinking carefully about the words they use, and by avoiding using the same word over and over again.
- One word that is often overused is *said*. Write the following sentence on the board, reminding the children about speech marks:
    "Where are you going?" said Jim.
- Encourage the children to think of the different ways Jim might ask his question. Ask the children what different words could be used in place of *said* in this sentence.
- Words that could be used instead of said include: *asked*, *replied*, *called*, *shouted*, *cried*, *whispered*, *roared*, *murmured*, *explained*, *yelled*, *screamed*, *answered*, *muttered*, *wondered*, *hissed*.

Activity Page
- The children look at the first word web on their page and read the word in its centre: *said*. In each section of this word web, the children write a word that could be used instead of *said*.
- The children complete the remaining word webs in the same way, finding synonyms for *sad*, and then *cold*.

- Encourage the children to look in storybooks for more examples of synonyms.

Extension Activity
- Provide some thesauruses for the children to look at and read.

Rounding Off
- See how many different words the children have thought of or found. Collate all the children's words and make a big class word web for the classroom wall.

Spelling: the ‹ur› spelling of the /er/ sound

Spelling Test
- The children turn to page 79 of their *Pupil Books* and find the column labelled *Spelling Test 33*.
- In no particular order, call out the spelling words the children learnt last week:
  yet, hid, wept, skirt, girl, shirt, first, of, eight, birthday.
- The children write these words on the lines for *Spelling Test 33*.

Revision
- Use flash cards to revise the spelling patterns taught so far. Use the flash cards, or the *Tricky Word Wall Flowers*, to revise the sixth set of tricky words

Letter Sound
- Remind the children that the main ways of writing the /er/ sound are ‹er›, ‹ir› and ‹ur›. Revise the ‹ur› spelling of the /er/ sound.
- With the children, make a list of words that use the ‹ur› spelling of the /er/ sound and write them on the board. (See word bank on page 26.) Ask the children to make up sentences using some of the words. Point out that two days of the week, *Saturday* and *Thursday,* use the ‹ur› spelling of the /er/ sound.
- The ‹ur› words could also be written onto a big turkey shape, which can then be used as a word bank for display.

Spelling List
- Read the spelling words with the children. As a class, say the sounds in the regular words, and say the letter names in the tricky words *love* and *cover*.
- The last word in the list, *hamburger*, is a compound word. The children will find this word easier to spell if they split the word up into its three syllables, 'ham', 'bur' and 'ger'. Point out that the /er/ sound in the middle of the word is spelt ‹ur›, but at the end of the word, the /er/ sound is spelt ‹er›.

not
sum
next
turn
nurse
turkey
purple
love
cover
hamburger

Activity Page
- Practise the joined ‹ur› formation. The children write inside the outline ‹ur› on their page using the correct formation. This can be done several times using different colours.
- The children write a ‹ur› word in each turkey. They draw pictures to illustrate each word. Encourage the children to write and colour neatly. Colouring helps the children to develop their pencil control.

Dictation
- Read the words one at a time. The children listen for the sounds in each word, and write the words on the lines.

  1. fur   2. burn
  3. hurt   4. burst
  5. curly 6. turning
  7. The nurse visits on Thursday.
  8. We always burn the toast.
  9. It is your turn next.

- Read the sentences one at a time for the children to write down. Remind the children that sentences start with a capital letter and end with a full stop.

Grammar: Questions

Aim
- To develop the children's understanding of questions, and to help them work out when to use question marks.

Introduction
- The children sit in a circle.
- Write the months of the year on the board, ensuring that all the children can see them. Read the months with the children.
- Go round the circle, with each child in turn saying the next month. Then go round the circle again, asking each child in turn 'When is your birthday?'

Main Point
- Write the question 'When is your birthday?' on the board.
- Ask the children if they know what the mark at the end of the sentence is. Explain that it is a question mark, and that it tells us that this sentence is a question. Show the children how to write a question mark.
- Write the ‹wh› question words on the board: *what*, *why*, *when*, *where*, *who* and *which*. Read the words with the children.
- Usually, when we ask a question, we expect an answer. Explain that questions can be used to get information. The children learnt when each other's birthdays were by asking the question 'When is your birthday?' Ask them to imagine meeting someone for the first time. What other questions could they ask to find out more about that person?

Activity Page
- Look at the activity page with the children, and read the question words. The children write inside the outlined question words using coloured pencils.
- They practise the formation of the question mark by tracing inside the outlined question marks on their page. Remind the children to start at the top when writing a question mark.
- The children answer the three questions about themselves.
- Next, they think of some questions they could ask someone they had just met, to find out more about that person.

Extension Activity
- The children think of as many questions as they can. They could take turns asking questions with a partner.

Rounding Off
- Go round the class, asking the children for their questions.

Spelling: the ‹au› spelling of the /or/ sound

Spelling Test
- The children turn to page 79 of their *Pupil Books* and find the column labelled *Spelling Test 34*.
- In no particular order, call out the spelling words the children learnt last week:
  not, sum, next, turn, nurse, turkey, purple, love, cover, hamburger.
- The children write these words on the lines for *Spelling Test 34*.

Revision
- Use flash cards to revise the spelling patterns taught so far, and the sixth set of tricky words

Letter Sound
- Remind the children that the main ways of writing the /or/ sound are ‹or› and ‹al›. Revise the ‹al› spelling of the /or/ sound.
- Explain to the children that the /or/ sound can also be written ‹au›. Write the word *August* on the board and explain that the ‹au› at the beginning of this word makes an /or/ sound. Ask the children if they can think of any other words in which ‹au› makes an /or/ sound.
- With the children, make a list of words that use the ‹au› spelling and write them on the board. Ask the children to make up sentences using some of the words. The ‹au› words could also be written onto a big astronaut shape, which can then be used as a word bank for display.
- There are not many ‹au› words. However, a few suitable examples are included in the word bank on page 26.

Spelling List
- Read the spelling words with the children. As a class, say the sounds in the regular words, and say the letter names in the tricky words *after* and *every*.
- The last word in the list, *astronaut*, is longer than the rest. The children will find this word easier to spell if they split the word up into its three syllables, 'ast', 'ro' and 'naut'.

map
fix
jump
fault
pause
haunt
August
after
every
astronaut

Activity Page
- Practise the joined ‹au› formation. The children write inside the outline ‹au› on their page using the correct formation. This can be done several times using different colours.
- The children write an ‹au› word in each astronaut. They draw pictures to illustrate each word. Encourage the children to write and colour neatly. Colouring helps the children to develop their pencil control.

Dictation
- Read the words one at a time. The children listen for the sounds in each word, and write the words on the lines.
- Read the sentences one at a time for the children to write down. Remind the children that sentences start with a capital letter and end with a full stop.

1. haul 2. fault
3. haunt 4. August
5. launch 6. vault
7. They always go there in August.
8. It was her fault.
9. Once I saw an astronaut.

Grammar: Questions

Aim
- To develop the children's understanding and use of questions.

Introduction
- Ask the children some questions, for example, 'What is your favourite colour?' 'Where did you go on holiday?' 'Who is your best friend?' 'When is your birthday?' 'Which drink do you like better, orange or blackcurrant?'
- Revise the ‹wh› question words, and write them on the board: *what, why, when, where, who* and *which*.
- Write questions on the board with the question words missing.
- For example:
    '_____ *do you live?*'   (Answer: where)
    '_____ *is your party?*'   (Answer: when)
    '_____ *likes chocolate?*' (Answer: who)
- Ask which question word would fit in each sentence. With the children, try inserting each of the questions words in turn, to see if they make sense.

Main Point
- Show the children some pictures of animals. Ask one child to choose an animal, but not to say which one they have chosen. The others ask questions to find out which animal it is.
- Remind the children that questions are usually asked to get information. The children will need to think carefully about which questions to ask, so that they find out as much as possible about the animal. The children must not guess which it is, until five questions have been asked.
- This is a simplified version of the game 20 questions. It can be played in spare moments.

Activity Page
- Read through the activity page with the class. The children complete each question by writing a ‹wh› question word in the gap. Their chosen word must make sense in the sentence.
- For the next activity, the children read the questions and the girl's answers, and try to work out which of the animals the girl is pretending to be.

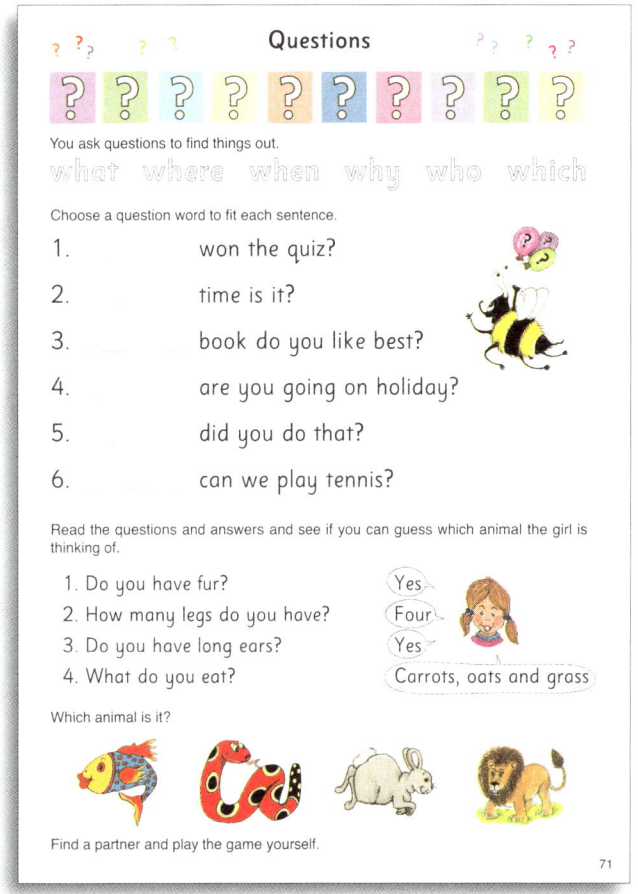

Extension Activity
- The children play the *What am I?* game in pairs.

Rounding Off
- Go over the activity page with the children.

Spelling: the ‹aw› spelling of the /or/ sound

Spelling Test
- The children turn to page 79 of their *Pupil Books* and find the column labelled *Spelling Test 35*.
- In no particular order, call out the spelling words the children learnt last week:
  map, fix, jump, fault, autumn, haunt, August, after, every, astronaut.
- The children write these words on the lines for *Spelling Test 35*.

Revision
- Use flash cards to revise the spelling patterns taught so far, and the sixth set of tricky words

Letter Sound
- Remind the children that the main ways of writing the /or/ sound are ‹or›, ‹al› and ‹au›. Revise the ‹al› and ‹au› spellings of the /or/ sound.
- Explain to the children that the /or/ sound can also be written ‹aw›. Remind the children that the ‹aw› in the tricky word *saw* makes an /or/ sound. Ask the children if they can think of any other words in which ‹aw› makes an /or/ sound.
- With the children, make a list of words that use the ‹aw› spelling and write them on the board. Ask the children to make up sentences using some of the words.
- The ‹aw› words could also be written onto a big saw shape, which can then be used as a word bank for display.
- There are not many ‹aw› words. However, a few suitable examples are included in the word bank on page 26.

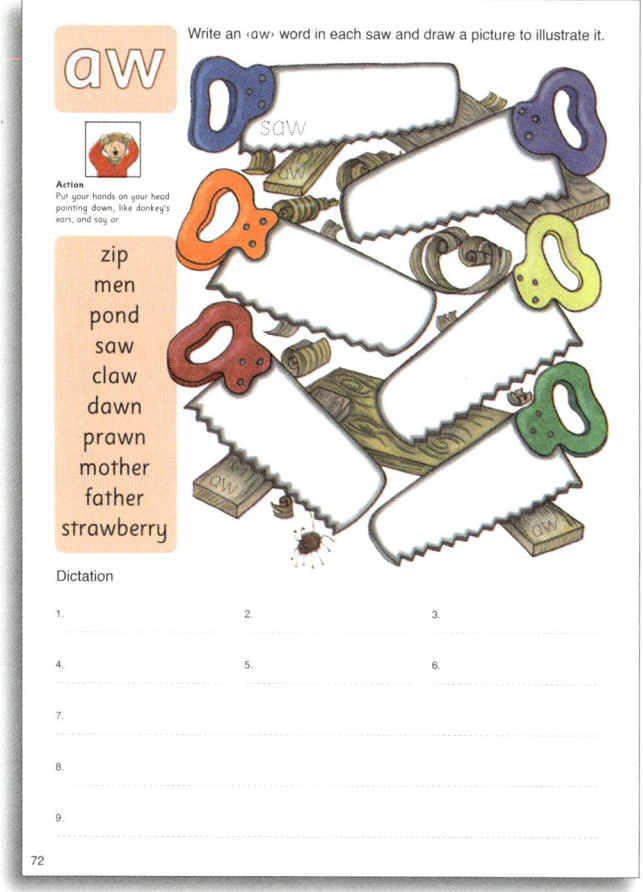

Activity Page
- Practise the joined ‹aw› formation. The children write inside the outline ‹aw› on their page using the correct formation. This can be done several times using different colours.
- The children write an ‹aw› word in each saw. They draw pictures to illustrate each word. Encourage the children to write and colour neatly. Colouring helps the children to develop their pencil control.

Spelling List
- Read the spelling words with the children. As a class, say the sounds in the regular words, and say the letter names in the tricky words *mother* and *father*.
- The last word in the list, *strawberry*, is a compound word. The children will find this word easier to spell if they split the word up into its three syllables, 'straw', 'ber' and 'ry'.

zip
men
pond
saw
claw
dawn
prawn
mother
father
strawberry

Dictation
- Read the words one at a time. The children listen for the sounds in each word, and write the words on the lines.
- Read the sentences one at a time for the children to write down. Remind the children that sentences start with a capital letter and end with a full stop.

1. raw	2. claw
3. thaw	4. drawn
5. shawl	6. straw
7. Try not to yawn.	
8. The cows lie down on some straw.	
9. Would you like some prawns?	

Grammar: Revision

Aim
- Revise the parts of speech learnt so far.

Introduction
- Revise proper nouns, common nouns and pronouns.
- Revise adjectives.
- Call out some nouns and ask the children to think of suitable adjectives to describe them.
- Revise verbs. Conjugate a verb.
- Revise adverbs. Call out some verbs and ask the children to think of suitable adverbs to describe them.

Main Point
- This is a revision session, which allows the children to apply some of the knowledge they have learnt to a piece of writing.
- Look at the last page in the *Jolly Grammar Big Book 1*. If this book is not available, choose a page from an alternative big book.
- Read the page with the children, identifying the parts of speech they have learnt.
- A large sheet of acetate could be placed over the page and used to underline the words in the appropriate colours.

Activity Page
- With the children, read the story on their *Pupil Book* page.
- First, the children write inside the outlined word *nouns* in black, and underline all the nouns they can find in the same colour.
- Then they write inside the outlined word *verbs* in red, and underline all the verbs they can find in the same colour.
- It does not matter if the children do not find all the nouns and verbs, so long as they see some of them and show that they are beginning to understand how words work in sentences.

Extension Activity
- The children repeat the exercise, identifying the pronouns, adjectives and adverbs.
- Pronouns should be underlined in pink, adjectives in blue and adverbs in orange.

Rounding Off
- Read through the activity page with the children, identifying the parts of speech. (See answers below.)

Inky toils long and hard in the garden. She digs the brown earth. The birds watch her interestedly. They wait eagerly for the grubs.

In the spring, Inky plants the seeds in the ground. She grows orange carrots, crispy lettuces and tall, green beans. In summer, she carefully harvests the yummy vegetables and eats them.

Inky also grows tall, yellow sunflowers in the garden. She likes the lovely sunflowers. The birds also like the sunflowers. They hungrily eat the striped black and white seeds.

- Only the parts of speech that the children have been taught are underlined in the passage above. Strictly speaking, *the* and *a* can be classed as adjectives, and *them* is a pronoun, but the children are not expected to know this at this stage.

The Grammar Handbook 2

The teaching in *The Grammar Handbook 2* follows on from the teaching in the *Jolly Grammar 1 Pupil* and *Teacher's Books*. This handbook covers the next year of grammar and spelling teaching.

With *The Grammar Handbook 2* the children are introduced to new parts of speech, including prepositions, conjunctions and possessive adjectives. Comparatives and superlatives are also introduced, and are explained in a child-friendly way. Proof reading activities give the children the opportunity to practise using dictionaries and thesauruses, and cloze activities help them to develop their comprehension skills. The weekly spelling activities help the children to reinforce the spelling knowledge they gained with the *Jolly Grammar 1* programme, as well as introducing more complex spelling patterns.